Quick Study Commentary Series:
Galatians and Ephesians

Chad Sychtysz

© 2024 Spiritbuilding Publishers.
All rights reserved. No part of this book may be reproduced in any form without the written permission of the publisher.

Published by
Spiritbuilding Publishers
9700 Ferry Road, Waynesville, Ohio 45068

QUICK STUDY COMMENTARY SERIES:
Galatians and Ephesians
By Chad Sychtysz

ISBN: 978-1-96480-505-4

Spiritbuilding
PUBLISHERS

spiritbuilding.com

Table of Contents

Quick Study Commentary—Galatians

Introduction to *Galatians* 1
Section One: Paul Defends His Authority (1:1—2:21) 9
Paul's Rebuke of the Galatians' Fickleness (1:1–10) 9
Paul's Personal History and Credentials (1:11–24) 13
Paul in Jerusalem (2:1–10) 17
Paul's Confrontation with Peter (2:11–21) 20
Section Two: Salvation by Grace vs. Justification by Law (3:1—4:31) ... 24
The True "Children of Abraham" (3:1–14) 24
The Purpose of the Law (3:15–29) 28
Paul's Personal Appeal to the Galatians (4:1–20) 33
The Allegory of Two Women (4:21–31) 38
Section Three: Led by the Spirit vs. Living by the Flesh (5:1—6:18) ... 42
Freedom Is Found in Christ, Not in Law (5:1–15) 42
Contrast of the Two Lifestyles (5:16–26) 47
Expectations for Those Led by the Spirit (6:1–10) 55
Concluding Remarks (6:11–18) 59
Sources Used for Galatians 62

Quick Study Commentary—Ephesians

Introduction to *Ephesians* 64
Section One: Praise to God for His Church (1:1–23) 69
Salutation (1:1–2) 69
Hymn of Praise to God (1:3–14) 69
Paul's First Prayer for the Ephesians (1:15–23) 75
Section Two: Universal Salvation in Christ (2:1—3:21) 79
Salvation by Grace through Faith (2:1–10) 79
The "One New Man" in Christ (2:11–22) 83
Paul's Ministry to the Revealed Gospel (3:1–13) 89
Paul's Second Prayer for the Ephesians (3:14–21) 93
Section Three: The Unity of Christ's Body (4:1–16) 98
The Unity of the Spirit (4:1–6) 98
God's Gifts to His Church (4:7–16) 102

Section Four: The Christian's Walk (4:17—6:9) **109**
Putting on the "New Self" (4:17–24) 109
Not That, But This (4:25—5:21) 112
The Marriage Relationship (5:22–33) 124
Other Relationships (6:1–9) 129
Section Five: The Christian's Struggle with the Unseen World (6:10–20)...134
Concluding Remarks (6:21–24) 138
Sources Used for *Ephesians* 140

Introduction to *Galatians*

The *Epistle to the Galatians* was not written to any one congregation, but to a group of churches in a region called Galatia. There has been controversy as to whether "Galatia" refers to the cultural region of Galatia (originally settled hundreds of years before Christ by Gauls from the north) or the Roman political province of Galatia. In either case, Galatia was in the middle of the Anatolian Peninsula (or central modern-day Turkey). Phrygia, Pontus, Bithynia, and Cappadocia bordered this region. Most scholars agree that Paul wrote *at least* to the churches in the southern portion of that area—specifically, those churches which he and Barnabas had established on their first missionary journey, namely, in Iconium, Lystra, and Derbe (Acts 14:1–28, 16:6, and 18:23). While some scholars propose that Paul wrote to northern Galatia (thus, the cities of Pessinus, Ancyra, and Tavium), there is nothing in *Acts* or other New Testament (NT) writings to prove Paul ever preached in the northern province of Galatia.[1]

Galatians is among the first letters—if not *the* first letter—written by Paul (that we know of) that circulated among the early churches. Paul wrote it around AD 50–51, shortly after the council in Jerusalem (Acts 15). He may have written it from Corinth during Paul's second missionary journey, though some believe it was written while he was in Antioch, immediately after that council. *Galatians* is often called "little Romans," since the main theses in *Galatians* are repeated and expounded upon extensively in that larger treatise. *Galatians* was a favorite book of the European Reformers (16–17th centuries), especially Martin Luther. These men saw a great similarity between Paul's confrontation with Judaists and their own confrontation with the Roman (Catholic) Church. William Ramsay calls *Galatians* "the most remarkable letter that ever was written."[2]

---

1   Nearly every commentator grapples with the "Who were the Galatians?" question, and the conclusion is nearly split on whether it refers to Northern or Southern Galatia. This study maintains that Paul wrote exclusively to churches in the Southern Galatian region, following the argument put forward by R. C. H. Lenski, *The Interpretation of St. Paul's Epistles to the Galatians, etc.* (Peabody, MA: Hendrickson Publishers, 1998), 8–12.

2   William Ramsay, *The Cities of St. Paul* (Whitefish, MT: Kessinger Publishing, 2004), 85.

No one has seriously doubted Paul's authorship of this letter. In fact, many have said that *Galatians* is the most Pauline composition one could imagine. Ramsay calls it "the most intensely individual of the Pauline Epistles."[3] The opening salutation (1:1), the first-person reference to the Jerusalem council and meetings with Peter and James (2:1–10), and allusions to the writer as being the apostle of the Gentiles, are unmistakably Pauline (compare with Rom. 15:15–19). This is supported by testimonies of the early church "fathers" and writers, which unanimously upheld Paul as the author of this epistle.[4] "No breath of suspicion as to the authorship, integrity or apostolic authority of the Epistle to the Galatians has reached us from ancient times."[5] Another scholar says: "[Paul] regarded his authority as the privilege rather than as the basis of his service. Since he had served the Galatian people by bringing them the message of the gospel, he used his apostolic office to demand a respectful hearing for what he still had to say to them."[6]

Purpose and Theme: The central issue which Paul addresses in *Galatians* is that Judaism cannot impose upon Gentile converts to Christianity. A Judaizer—a term used in studies of *Galatians*—refers to one who strictly imposed the Law of Moses, especially in the context of proselytes.[7] Judaism

---

3   Ibid., 4.

4   Robert Jamieson, Andrew Fausset and David Brown. *Commentary Critical and Explanatory on the Whole Bible (1871)* (database © 2012 by WORDsearch Corp.); on "Introduction."

5   George G. Findlay, "Galatians, Epistle to," *The International Standard Bible Encyclopedia*, vol. 2 (Grand Rapids: Eerdmans Publishing Co., 1939), 1156.

6   Merrill C. Tenney, *Galatians: The Charter of Christian Liberty* (Grand Rapids: Wm. B. Eerdmans Publishing Co., 1957), 43.

7   "Circumcision" meant more than the mere cutting of the flesh, but often encompassed the Judaic belief system. Thus, when Paul refers to circumcision as a religious practice (as in 5:3), he means the Law of Moses; "A man placed himself under the entire Mosaic system by submitting to circumcision" (Lenski, 254). But several commentators believe that only circumcision (and perhaps a few other ordinances, such as Sabbath-keeping, diet, etc.) was the full objective of the Judaizers (William Hendriksen, *New Testament Commentary: Galatians, Ephesians, etc.* [Grand Rapids: Baker Books, 1995], 19). Incidentally, "Judaists" and "Judaizers" mean the same thing and can be used interchangeably. "The term [Judaizer] is derived from a coined Latin word *Iudaizo* meaning 'to be or live like a Jew.' It is a religious designation rather than a national description" (L. M. Petersen, "Galatians, Epistle to," *The Zondervan Biblical Encyclopedia* [Grand Rapids: Zondervan, 1976], 631). That author also refers to Judaizers as "Old Testament Christians," which is an interesting way of characterizing these men.

typically went well beyond the Law of Moses, however, for it married the Law given to Israel at Sinai with long-held rabbinical traditions. The Judaist believed that these traditions were as authoritative as the Law itself—an erroneous belief that Jesus Himself brought to their attention (Mat. 15:1–6, Mark 7:5–13). As Judaists became Christians, they sometimes brought with them their proud heritage, deep-seated reverence for the Law, and a self-righteousness based upon law-keeping rather than divine grace. Thus, some Jews who had believed were insistent that the Law be compulsory for new converts (Acts 15:5). If this ideology/theology was true, then the following would also be true:

- The Law of Moses is still binding as a legal imposition upon all believers.
- The Law is just as important and necessary as the gospel.
- All Gentiles who become disciples of Christ would also have to become disciples of Moses (as the Judaists proudly considered themselves; see John 9:27–28).
- Just as Gentile converts to Judaism were considered (in essence) second-class citizens—since they could never be *Jews*—so Gentile converts to Christ are still regarded as inferior to Jewish Christians.
- This would impose a two-tier system within the church—which would conflict with the unifying and barrier-removing work of Christ (see Eph. 2:13–18).
- All the work that Paul (and others) had done among the Gentiles would be compromised by these facts; many Gentiles might abandon the gospel by mistakenly seeing it as just another brand of Jewish religion.
- Paul (and other ministers to the Gentiles) would be regarded not only as opponents of (the Law of) Moses but also guilty of having taught Gentile believers only *part* of the gospel of Christ.
- Paul's authority and authenticity as an apostle of Christ would be irreparably damaged, and he would lose all credibility *as* an apostle among both Jews and Gentiles.
- Gentile churches would recognize the Judaizers—and not Christ's hand-picked apostles—as the leading authorities in the churches and would be free to teach Judaism alongside the teaching of Christ.

These are the serious doctrinal issues that prompted the so-called council of Jerusalem (Acts 15). They also help us to understand why Paul himself so aggressively resisted the Judaizing teachers in that council as well as in his missionary efforts and his epistles to various churches. Paul understood this contest as a major turning point for the church; its outcome would forever determine the effectiveness of the gospel among the non-Jewish world. (It is important to note that not *all* believing Jews shared the views of Judaizers.)

The Judaizers did not see themselves as the enemy of the gospel, however. They saw themselves as genuine keepers of what was sacred to God. They would not accept the fact that God would (in their minds) *abandon* the Law for another means of salvation. More specifically, they struggled to comprehend—or outright resisted—the idea that a person could be saved by grace *apart from* keeping the sacred commandments given to Israel on Mt Sinai.[8] Such beliefs, fanned by human pride and Jewish nationalism, prevented many Jews from becoming Christians; some of those who *did* convert to Christianity refused to let go of these views. To them, the only way God would justify a person was through his law-keeping. In effect, Christianity was merely a steppingstone; Judaism was the ultimate objective.

While the Judaizing teachers may have made a convincing argument to some—including the Galatian converts—Paul saw their seemingly pious stance as arrogant and heretical. It was impossible, he maintained, to have *ever* been justified by works (of law); God has *always* saved men by divine grace in response to genuine human faith. In other words, the Judaizers were not only wrong to marry Judaism with the gospel of Christ but have been wrong about law-keeping all along (see Rom. 10:1–4). Physical performance or human effort cannot rectify the spiritual problem of sin. Law-keeping *at best* is an act of faith, not an act of self-justification. Likewise, the healing of a person's soul through "works of law" are not *on par with* divine intervention (Gal. 3:3). Either a person is saved by divine grace or by perfect, flawless law-keeping; once he has sinned against the law, however, he is no longer a law-keeper but a lawbreaker. No lawbreaker, then, can redeem himself in his own corrupted state of being. By choosing to be justified by law—whether the Law of Moses or any self-imposed works of human effort—a person nullifies the power of God's saving grace for himself (5:2–4).

---

8   This is the meaning of "apart from law" statements in Paul's letters; see Rom. 3:21, 28, for example.

The Judaizers had considerable sway over the Gentiles, however. Paul called this influence a "bewitching"—not a wholesome persuasion but one involving a self-serving and sinister agenda (3:1). Apparently the Galatians were fond of mystic religion (of the Mother-Goddess Cybele, in neighboring Phrygia) and thus believed that "the full privileges of Christianity could only be attained through an elaborate system of ceremonial symbolism"—namely, circumcision and the other rites of the Law of Moses.[9] In other words, the Judaizing teachers appealed to their sense of resting upon human *performance* as a means of achieving spiritual wisdom and moral righteousness. They may have also heard that Paul seemed a supporter of the Law when he was with Jews but appeared to renounce it when with Gentiles. The persuasion of the Judaizing teachers, then, was to portray Paul as a false representative of the gospel of Christ: he did not accurately teach the Jerusalem apostles' version of the gospel but his own; he purposely denied Gentiles their right to enjoy what Jewish Christians enjoyed (even though they did not see the ulterior motives involved); he was a flatterer and renegade teacher, not a genuine apostle.

These insinuations—and the serious damage that they presented to Paul's credibility and ministry among the Gentiles—had to be immediately refuted. This explains the blunt and reproving tone of much of this epistle. "He wrote to the Galatians an Epistle which begins with an abruptness and severity showing his sense of the urgency of the occasion, and the greatness of the danger. It is also frequently characterised [sic] by a tone of sadness, such as would naturally be felt by a man of such warm affections when he heard that those whom he loved were forsaking his cause and believing the calumnies of his enemies."[10] It was the Judaists who were falsely representing the gospel, not Paul; it was they who denied Gentiles the full rights and privileges of the gospel, not Paul; and it was they who enslaved these people to their self-serving brand of Christianity, not Paul.

Several times throughout the epistle, Paul expresses amazement, perplexity, and sheer disappointment with the Galatian converts (1:6, 3:1, 4:11, 5:7,

---

9   JFB, *Commentary* (electronic), on "Introduction"; Hendriksen, *NTC*, 5; and Ramsay, *Cities*, 330.

10 W. J. Conybeare and J. S. Howson, *The Life and Epistles of St. Paul* (Grand Rapids: Eerdmans Publishing Co., 1964), 478.

etc.). The Judaizers privately believed it was beneath them to be on the same spiritual plane of Gentiles; they would allow Gentiles to ascend to their level but would always maintain the upper hand. In sharp contrast, Paul argues the equalizing effect of both sin *and* the gospel: just as all people—Jews and Gentiles—are condemned because of sin, so all people are saved by Christ. Those who are saved are *equals* "in Christ": from heaven's perspective, there are no distinctions between Jews and Gentiles, masters and servants, or male and female (3:28). "For you are all sons of God through faith in Christ Jesus" (3:26)—there is no two-party, two-tier, or clergy-laity system in the Lord's church. One does not obtain perfection and freedom by works of law but through faith in Christ (1:3–4, 3:3, and 5:1).

Galatians is comprised of three general sets of arguments that refute the false charges of the Judaizers *and* clarify the true teaching of the gospel:

- Apostolic authority (chapters 1—2). The gospel Paul preached did not come from men (or the twelve apostles) but directly from God by way of divine revelation (1:10–12).
- Accusations concerning Paul's alleged flip-flop position on the Law of Moses (chapters 3—4). The Law was a tutor designed to lead Jews to the gospel of Christ and was never meant to be permanent (3:24). Christ, not the Law, is the fulfillment of God's promise to Abraham.
- Accusations that Paul was leading the Galatians down his own path rather than closer to God (chapters 5—6). Christians are led by the Spirit, not by men (5:16); they are justified by faith in God, not by works of law (or, human effort). This Spirit-led life will be evidenced by "fruit" which is consistent with the nature of God—not physical manifestations (such as circumcision, ceremonial rites, etc.).

Because much of *Galatians* deals with a contest between Judaism and genuine Christianity, the contemporary reader might view this letter as outdated and irrelevant. This is hardly the case. It is far more accurate to say that *Galatians* deals with the most important and relevant issues of all— namely, how sinful people are justified by a Righteous God. Instead of being archaic or "ancient history," *Galatians* outlines the basic concerns of people and their relationship with God. It addresses the fallacy that human effort (law-keeping) can duplicate or replace divine redemption (divine grace).

It also puts the emphasis on Christ and *His* work rather than Christians and *their* work(s). These are issues with which people within the church continue to struggle even today. Some of the highlights of this letter include:

- Left to themselves, people gravitate from truth to fallacy (1:6–9).
- God justifies human souls by grace, not works of men (2:11–21).
- Christ's atonement is sufficient for all human sin (2:15–16).
- God has revealed His gospel to those whom He chose for this purpose (2:6, 10).
- The gospel expounds upon the relationship between legal requirements of law and spiritual freedom (2:17–21).
- The gospel provides a proper context and understanding of God's covenant with Israel and the Law of Moses (3:15–18, 4:21–31).
- All men and women are—as children of God—equal "in Christ" (3:27–29).
- Christ's church is united through "faith working through love," not people working their way to self-justification (5:1–6).
- The Holy Spirit is the guiding force within Christians, not the imposition of laws, rites, or ceremonial distinctions (5:16, 25).
- Christians are not in competition with each other but are to help and restore one another as needed (5:26, 6:1–2).

General Outline of *Galatians*

- ❏ Introduction to *Galatians*
- ❏ Section One: Paul Defends His Authority (1:1—2:21)
  - Paul's Rebuke of the Galatians' Fickleness (1:1–10)
  - Paul's Personal History and Credentials (1:11–24)
  - Paul's Confrontation with Peter (2:11–21)
- ❏ Section Two: Salvation by Grace versus Justification by Law (3:1—4:31)
  - The True "Children of Abraham" (3:1–14)
  - The Purpose of the Law (3:15–29)
  - Paul's Personal Appeal to the Galatians (4:1–20)
  - The Allegory of Two Women (4:21–31)
- ❏ Section Three: Led by the Spirit versus Living by the Flesh (5:1—6:18)
  - Freedom is Found in Christ, Not in Law (5:1–15)
  - Contrast of the Two Lifestyles (5:16–26)
  - Expectations for Those Led by the Spirit (6:1–10)
  - Concluding Remarks (6:11–18)

SECTION ONE:
PAUL DEFENDS HIS AUTHORITY
(1:1—2:21)

Paul's Rebuke of the Galatians' Fickleness
(Gal. 1:1–10)

Paul begins his epistle by unequivocally stating his authority (1:1), but he does so by way of a disclaimer—in essence, "I am this, but not that."[11] "Apostle" means "one sent, an envoy; ambassador."[12] The One who "sent" Paul was not a man or any human agency; it was Jesus Christ *and* God the Father. As God raised Christ from the grave, so He has the power and authority to raise up a man like Paul as an apostle.[13] In other words, Paul is not some upstart, renegade, or rogue preacher who claims to have authority (but really does not). He is a genuine apostle, commissioned by God Himself, and capable of defending his apostleship with revealed knowledge and miraculous signs (2 Cor. 12:12). If his apostleship is genuine, then so is the gospel that he preaches. "[A]nd all the brethren who are with me" (1:2)—implying that those outside of Galatia were convinced of his credentials.

"To the churches of Galatia" (1:2) indicates that the problems Paul addresses in this epistle were not limited to one congregation but had infected an entire region. Peter also addressed this group of churches in his

---

11   "Why the disclaimer? None of his other letters following the affirmation of his apostleship contain this defensive qualification. ... We deduce ... that the false teachers' *modus operandi*, which was necessary for them to superimpose their teaching on the apostle's teaching, was to discredit both Paul's person and apostleship. By this means they had effectively overcome the Galatians' strong fraternity for Paul (4:14–15), as well as his apostolic authority. This explains Paul's disclaimer and why he stressed his divine appointment to the apostleship" (Edward C. Wharton, *Freed for Freedom: Studies in Galatians* [Nashville, TN: 21st Century Christian, 1995], 45).

12   Joseph Thayer, *Thayer's Greek Definitions* (electronic version) (database © 2014 by WORDsearch Corp.), G652.

13   In John 10:18, Jesus said He would raise Himself from the dead; in Rom. 8:11, Paul claims that the power of the Holy Spirit raised Jesus from the dead; here in Gal. 1:1, the Father raised His Son. All three assertions are correct, since it was *God's power* that raised Jesus from the grave, and all three of the Godhead possess this power.

general epistle (1 Peter 1:1). The absence of any personal or special words of commendation implies that Paul is anxious—even as he pens this letter—to get to the point as soon as possible. Even so, he does not refuse to pass up an opportunity to express his adoration of Jesus Christ (1:3–5). This praise serves another purpose as well: the emphasis on what *Jesus* does for believers is paramount to what believers do for Him. This seems purposely stated, since the Judaizing teachers preached a gospel of human effort and works of law rather than a dependence upon the grace of God. The "present evil age," then, would refer not only to the world of the unconverted but also alludes to those who pervert the gospel of Christ. "There is no deliverance from the evils of the world until we are delivered from our sins. Sin is the cause of the evil of the world."[14]

The Galatians' Inexplicable Behavior (1:6–9): "I am amazed [or, I marvel]" (1:6)—Paul responds with genuine perplexity toward the Galatians' fickle behavior. God calls them and they listen and respond; some man "calls" them and they give him equal attention and devotion! "So quickly" means "in a short period of time," not necessarily immediately after Paul had left them. They had so quickly abandoned the doctrinal teachings of the gospel—a gospel of *grace*, not works and self-justification—and had patterned themselves after certain influential teachers. (The Greek verb tense here indicates ongoing action: "you are *continuing* to desert Him."[15]) One does not have access to the Father through meritorious works of human effort but a holy calling by the grace of God (Eph. 2:18, 2 Thess. 2:13–14). Saving grace is everything God does for the believer that *he cannot do for himself* regarding salvation.[16] While human works are necessary to demonstrate human faith (James 2:14–26), such works can never compare to or replace the work of divine grace.

A "different gospel" (1:6) means one that Paul did not deliver to them. The gospel that the Judaizing teachers preached to the Galatians was like what Paul preached, yet crucial differences made theirs ungenuine, lacking in

---

14   David Lipscomb, *A Commentary on the New Testament Epistles: Second Corinthians and Galatians* (Nashville: Gospel Advocate Co., 1979), 188.

15   JFB, *Commentary* (electronic), on 1:6.

16   For a further study on "grace," I strongly recommend my book, *The Gospel of Saving Grace* (Spiritbuilding Publishers, 2020); go to www.spiritbuilding.com/chad.

authority, and filled with contradictions. "[W]hich is really not another" (1:7)—i.e., not another of the same kind; not an equal and acceptable alternative. "Paul was saying that the Galatians had listened to a totally different gospel, though there is really no other gospel than the one he preached."[17] Theirs was a distortion [lit., perversion] of the only authentic revelation from God—and those who preached it were impostors, not apostles (cf. 2 Cor. 11:13–14). "It is no 'gospel' (good news) at all, but a yoke of bondage to the law and the abolition of grace."[18]

Such men were "disturbing" the Galatians by filling their heads with convoluted messages and contradictory teachings.[19] These teachers had received no revelations from God but acted as though they had; they were not promoters of sound doctrine but wanted to impose their beliefs upon others (cf. 1 Tim. 6:3–5). The "gospel of Christ" means the full message of salvation by God through Jesus Christ. It is the *good news* of redemption which is not based upon the finite and fallible power of men but the infinite and infallible power of God (Rom. 1:16). "Paul's anger was aroused, not because he was jealous of rivals, but because the leaders of the dissenting party in Galatia were palming off a substitute for the gospel of Christ as the genuine article."[20]

In response to this, Paul pronounces one of the most strongly worded curses in the NT upon these Judaizing teachers. "But even if we, or an angel from heaven" (1:8)—i.e., while the gospel had come to the Galatians through Paul, he did not own the rights to it; this message was not his to amend or adjust according to his preferences. Likewise, not even *heavenly* messengers could preach something different. The gospel is "of Christ"—it is not just *about* Him, but He *owns* it and has full authority *over* it. One who dares to challenge that authority "is accursed"—lit., *anathema*, "a thing devoted to God without hope of being redeemed … therefore, a person or thing

---

17 JFB, *Commentary* (electronic), on 1:7.
18 A. T. Robertson, *Word Pictures in the New Testament*, vol. IV (Grand Rapids: Baker Book House [no date]), 276.
19 Hendriksen translates this (1:7), "Certain individuals are throwing you into confusion" (*NTC*, 40), which gives perhaps a clearer understanding than "disturbing you."
20 Tenney, *Galatians*, 56.

doomed to destruction."[21] To preach a false gospel *as though it were from God* is a crime of the highest order. It not only brings condemnation upon the one who preaches it, but it misleads an untold number of people who accept it as the truth (cf. Mat. 18:4–7). God cannot contradict Himself; Christ did not reveal two equally valid messages of salvation; the Holy Spirit does not speak out of both sides of His mouth.

The Judaizing teachers acted as if they had obtained their credentials from the apostles in Jerusalem. They asserted their alleged "authority" over and against Paul's; they imposed themselves upon those whom Paul had already led to Christ with the purity and simplicity of His gospel (2 Cor. 11:3). Paul taught that the Galatians gained freedom in Christ; the Judaizers then compelled these same people to keep the Law of Moses and its ceremonial rites. The misinformation and confusion caused by these illegitimate teachers was having devastating effects—not only for the Galatians but for all who would follow suit. The matter had to be countered quickly and directly; thus Paul minces no words in condemning it. "So I now say again" (1:9)—the seriousness of this matter warrants repeating heaven's denunciation of it. And if Paul so strongly condemns this *teaching*, the *reception* of it is also perilous.

Paul's Allegiance to Christ, Not Men (1:10): Clearly, Paul would not say such things if he was trying to please *men* rather than God (1:10). The Judaizers had accused Paul of flattering men to win their support; Paul bluntly refutes all such accusations. In essence, he says, "Why would I preach to you something that *I could not change* to gain popular approval? This does not make sense. You Galatians should be ashamed of yourselves for so quickly accepting such accusations against me."[22] The Jews were known to be men-pleasers, and especially the Pharisees (Luke 16:15, John 12:42–43). Paul states adamantly: "I do not share their agenda; I am not their servant; I serve Christ and Christ alone." "Bond-servant" [Greek, *doulos*] is translated

---

21 Thayer, *Definitions* (electronic), G331. The Old Testament phrase "under the ban" most closely identifies with the meaning here. Things devoted to God in this way were to be destroyed, without mercy or relenting; see Deut. 7:26, 13:17, Josh. 6:17–18, 7:15, etc.

22 The insulting nature of the Galatians "so quickly" abandoning Paul (as well as his teaching) is similar to that which he addresses with the Corinthians. Some of those people had not only reneged on their support of Paul, they also did not stand up to defend Paul against the accusations made against him.

elsewhere in the NT as "slave." Depending on the context, this servitude (or slavery) is either voluntary or involuntary; a person either willingly accepts it or someone forces it upon him. In the present case, Paul freely accepts his servitude to Christ even at the expense of his own unpopularity.

Paul's Personal History and Credentials (Gal. 1:11–24)

Paul's tone so far has been terse and blunt. As he begins to lay his own personal history before the Galatians, he relaxes this, appealing to them as "brethren" (1:11). The gospel he preached to them "is not according to man"—that is, it is not of human origin and therefore supersedes human authority. Paul "received" the gospel—not only the message itself but also the apostolic authority to declare it—"through a revelation of Jesus Christ" (1:12). This latter phrase can mean "a revelation that *concerns* Christ" or "that came directly *from* Christ"; in the present context, both meanings are equally valid (see 1 Cor. 2:1–5, 11:23, 15:3, Eph. 3:3, and 1 Thess. 4:15). Paul does not disclose the *conveyance* of this revelation. Certainly, the revelation began with Paul's (Saul's) conversion experience on the road to Damascus (Acts 9:1ff). Thereafter, he would receive divine information on an as-needed basis (Acts 18:9–10, 23:11, 27:23–24, etc.). But the core of this revelation seems to go far beyond such incidental disclosures.

Paul Recounts His Past (1:13–24): "For you have heard" (1:13–14)—no doubt from Paul himself but also from Barnabas and Christians who traveled through those churches.[23] While the Judaizers prided themselves on a militant devotion to the Law and to their heritage, Paul had eclipsed all his contemporaries. In the Pharisaic circles, Paul was a rising star who had sat at the feet of the great Rabbi Gamaliel (Acts 22:3, 23:6, and 26:5), groomed to be a great rabbi himself. While now he serves to build up the church, he once was a "persecutor and a violent aggressor" (1 Tim. 1:13)—and, at the time, proud of it. He did not simply try to discourage people from becoming

---

23 "The biographical data in Galatians were not written by Paul for the purpose of narrating interesting facts about himself but as a means of accounting for the stand which he took on the relation of the law and the gospel. He wanted to show to the Galatians that his message was not a pose which he had adopted for the sake of expediency or from a desire for notoriety, but that it sprang from a divine intervention in his own life" (Tenney, *Galatians*, 84–85).

Christians; he sought instead to destroy the church, believing that it stood in direct contradiction to the Law of Moses (Acts 22:4, 26:11, and Phil. 3:4–6). The Greek phrase "for my ancestral traditions" refers specifically to the traditions of one's father, grandfather, etc., rather than to national ancestry. "Paul's father was a strict Pharisee and had trained his son to be even stricter. The [Greek] adjective makes the impression that this Pharisaism was a trait of long standing in the family. Its proudest and most militant member was Saul."[24]

"But" (1:15–16a)—through a life-changing, history-altering, road-to-Damascus epiphany, Paul's career track to become a great Pharisee rabbi came to a screeching halt. God "set [Paul] apart from [his] mother's womb"—an expression meaning that his commission had been determined even before he was born. Yet it also refers to the path that God had allowed Paul to take in his life as a means of *preparing* him for this ministry. It might be said that for as long as the church had been in the mind of God, so too was a man like Paul to proclaim it. In other words, while Paul thought he was to become a great rabbi, God was grooming him to be a great apostle. William Ramsay has excellent comments on this:

> The choice of himself was the final execution of a design which had been long maturing in the purpose of God, and which was worked out step by step in the process of events. Already before his birth Paul had been chosen and set apart as the Apostle of the Gentiles; and, when the proper moment had arrived, the revelation took place, and the design of God was made consciously present in the mind and heart of man. It was not a sudden and incalculable choice of a human instrument. It was the consummation of a process of selection and preparation which had begun before the man was born, but of which he had at first been wholly unconscious—so unconscious that he had spent his energy in fighting vainly against its compelling power. Only in later time, as he reviewed his life, he could see the preparatory stages in the process, beginning before his birth; the purpose of God had matured its design by the selection through a long period of means useful to the ultimate end.[25]

---

24 Lenski, *Interpretation*, 53; bracketed word is mine.
25 Ramsay, *Cities*, 86.

"[C]alled me through His grace" reveals Paul's humility toward his own position: he knows he did not deserve it or had earned it; "but by the grace of God I am what I am" (1 Cor. 15:10). God "revealed His Son in [Paul]" through the indwelling of His Spirit (Rom. 8:9, Col. 1:29): the revelation was not only that of information and doctrine; it was personal and deeply sacred. While the twelve apostles focused predominantly (but not exclusively) on their ministry to the Jews, God appointed Paul as a minister to the Gentiles (Col. 1:25–28).[26]

Though a fellow apostle with them, Paul "did not immediately consult" with the twelve apostles in Jerusalem—or with anyone else—concerning his calling (1:16a–17). Instead, he retreated into relative isolation and obscurity, and nothing factually is known about this time of his life. During this time, God revealed to him whatever was necessary to prepare him for the ministry to come. It is likely that Paul pored over the Old Testament (OT) Scriptures with a completely new perspective. But beyond this we can only speculate. Just as the twelve apostles needed time (three years) to prepare for their own ministries, Paul also needed time for preparation and reflection. "Arabia" is a broad and ambiguous description for a large region of desert and wilderness areas to the north, east, and south of Palestine. In ancient times, Arabia often referred to the Sinai Peninsula, but this region juts northward into the southern regions of Mesopotamia (a.k.a. the Fertile Crescent) to the east of Syria. If we piece together what Luke records of Paul's early Christian history with what Paul also provides in *Galatians*, this is what appears to have happened:

- Paul was converted (ca. AD 35) in the several days between Christ's appearance to him and his baptism in Damascus (Acts 9:1–19).
- He spent "many days" in Damascus thereafter, preaching and teaching that Jesus is the Son of God, and practicing his new-found faith (Acts 9:20–22).
- After the Jews in Damascus had formed a plot against Paul's life, he escaped from that city and disappeared for awhile (Acts 9:23–25, 2 Cor.

---

26 Using wordplay, Paul makes a solemn point here (1:15). "Pharisee" is derived from *perisha*, "a separated (one)"; yet God "separated" Paul to his apostolic ministry even before he was recognized as a Pharisee. Thus, God made him a kind of "separated one" (in 1:15, *pharush*) in a higher sense than is possible according to the Jewish rabbis (Lenski, *Interpretation*, 56).

11:32–33).
- It appears at this point that Paul retreated into Arabia, both to contemplate his radical conversion and immerse himself in his studies and receive divine revelations (1:17). It is possible that at this time Paul received his vision of Paradise (2 Cor. 12:1–4). It is also reasonable to assume that the "Arabia" mentioned here refers to Syrian Arabia (because of its proximity to Damascus) rather than the Sinai Peninsula.
- After this time, Paul returned to Damascus—better trained and more prepared to deal with his ministry (1:17).
- "Three years later"—likely calculated from the time from his conversion in Damascus—Paul "went up to Jerusalem." Initially, he tried to fellowship with the church there, but they resisted him due to his past. It was not until Barnabas "took hold" of Paul and personally introduced him to "the apostles" that these men—Paul, Peter (Cephas), and James[27]—finally met each other (Acts 9:27). It was at that time that Paul spent "fifteen days" with Peter (1:18–19). (We assume that the other apostles were on missionary missions elsewhere, just as Peter himself later pursued in Acts 9:32ff.)
- While he was in Jerusalem, Paul spent time reasoning and debating with the Judaizers, and especially with the Hellenistic Jews—Greek-speaking, foreign-born Jews (as opposed to the Judean Jews who were born and raised in Jerusalem and its environs). These latter Jews, unable to reason against or accept what Paul taught (as with Stephen; see Acts 6:9–10), formed a plot against Paul's life, forcing him to leave Jerusalem.
- Paul then traveled northward into Syria, then westward into the Anatolian Peninsula into his own home region of Cilicia, and specifically to the city of Tarsus (Acts 9:30, Gal. 1:21).
- Paul remained in Tarsus for an indefinite period, until Barnabas sought him out for the work in Antioch of Syria (Acts 11:22–26).
- Paul continued to work in Antioch until the Holy Spirit called him and Barnabas (ca. AD 49–50) to embark on their missionary journey that led to the founding of the Galatian churches (Acts 13:1–3).

---

27 James, "the Lord's brother" (1:19), was not numbered with the twelve apostles, nor did he possess their power (2 Cor. 12:12) or apostolic authority. He did, however, wield considerable influence among the Jews in Jerusalem (see Acts 15:13ff and 21:18ff), likely because of his flesh-and-blood relation with Jesus. Thus, "apostles" in this sense is used in a general sense, just as when Barnabas is called an "apostle" (Acts 14:14).

Paul's did not stay long in Jerusalem, although he was no stranger to the city. While he was well-known among the Jewish leaders, he remained a relative stranger to the Christians in Judea (1:22–23). His reputation had preceded him; his conversion to the very belief system that he so aggressively tried to destroy could not be suppressed. "And they were glorifying God because of me" (1:24)—ironically, those who did not know Paul accepted him and his conversion as authentic; yet the Christians in Galatia that had met him and benefited from his work among them doubted his credibility.

Paul in Jerusalem (Gal. 2:1–10)

"Then after an interval of fourteen years" (2:1)—likely, Paul means here fourteen years since his conversion. Commentators are divided, however, as to which trip to Jerusalem is meant here. In Acts 11:29–30, the Christians in Antioch took up a collection for the famine-stricken saints in Jerusalem, and this money was sent by way of Paul and Barnabas. Some believe Paul is referring to this trip. Yet that visit to Jerusalem seems short and (according to Luke) uneventful (see Acts 12:25); there is nothing linking the one to the other. Paul had not yet been "set apart" by the Holy Spirit for his ministry to the Gentiles abroad.

Paul Recounts His Participation in the Council (2:1–10): The summit meeting in Jerusalem in Acts 15, however, seems much more plausible and relevant to Paul's discussion with the Galatians. The purpose for that meeting (or council) was to directly answer the question of whether to impose the Law of Moses upon Gentile converts; this is the same scenario with which Paul faces with the churches in Galatia. The meeting in Jerusalem would have put Paul in the spotlight since he was a prominent preacher to the Gentiles; this same intense focus upon Paul and his actions is what he describes in his letter to the Galatians. Paul went to Jerusalem "because of a revelation" (2:2); his participation in the council meeting would support this fact far more strongly than his conveyance of the funds from Antioch. It seems that the far greater weight of evidence links Acts 15 with Gal. 2. Until better evidence reveals otherwise, this study will continue with this conclusion.[28]

---

28 Hendriksen (*NTC*, 71–73) also offers a substantial and convincing argument in favor

This is the first (chronological) mention of Titus in the NT (2:1). (Paul mentions him several times in *2 Corinthians*, but that was written years after *Galatians*.) Paul has nothing but good things to say about this man. The way Paul uses him and relies upon him says a great deal concerning his respect for him. He later calls Titus "my partner and fellow worker" (2 Cor. 8:23) and "my true child in a common faith" (Titus 1:4). Such references lead us to believe that Paul had converted Titus, and he may be among the "some others" that accompanied Paul and Barnabas to Jerusalem (Acts 15:2).[29]

Before meeting with the entire assembly that would comprise the council, Paul first met privately with the leaders, namely, Peter, John, and James (see 2:9). The purpose of that meeting was to make certain that they were all in agreement before bringing the matter to a larger (and far more aggressive) audience. Paul's "fear" was that his ministerial work among the Gentiles would be "in vain" (2:2); therefore, he takes precaution in dealing with this sensitive and volatile situation. Yet the point Paul presses with the Galatians is: his authority is equal to that of the Jerusalem leaders, not in contradiction to it.

Since Titus was not a Jew, he was uncircumcised; his presence in Jerusalem during the council there intentionally pushed the envelope regarding the debate over the Law (2:3). Instead of succumbing to the pressure to circumcise Titus, Paul adamantly resists: "But we did not yield in subjection to them for even an hour" (2:3)—"them" being Pharisaic Jews who insisted upon compulsory observance of the Law of Moses. Circumcising Titus would have supported these Jews' position; it would have undermined the uniqueness of the gospel *and* would have made Gentiles subservient to the Jews. To clarify: these "false brethren" are not necessarily those Pharisaic Christians who were wrestling with the great transition from

---

of this view. Instead of repeating his points here, you are encouraged to read them in his own work.

29 Some believe the reason Titus is not mentioned in *Acts* is because he is Luke's brother, and Luke chose not to mention Titus for the same reason he may have chosen not to mention himself by name—likely, to avoid any accusations of self-promotion. Ramsey and other commentators have found this to be a reasonable explanation (Simon J. Kistemaker, *New Testament Commentary: Exposition of the Acts of the Apostles* [Grand Rapids: Baker Book House, 1990], 293–294; F. F. Bruce, *The Book of the Acts* [Grand Rapids: Eerdmans, 1964], 406; James Coffman, *Commentary on Acts* [Austin: Firm Foundation, 1977], 383; and others).

the Law to the gospel—i.e., "those who had believed" (Acts 15:5). Paul appears to refer to another group—an insidious handful of men who were *not* sincere Christians but portrayed themselves as such.[30] These men had been "secretly brought [into]" the council meeting to argue against Paul and Barnabas. Such men wanted to enslave the Gentiles with their own Law; this contradicted the message of freedom in Christ and "the truth of the gospel" (2:4).

Not only did Paul refuse to succumb to the impositions of these "false brethren," he also did not take orders from those who were genuine Christian leaders (2:6–10). These men had nothing on Paul; "For I consider myself not in the least inferior to the most eminent apostles" (2 Cor. 11:5). His parenthetical statement ("what they were makes no difference to me") is not meant to be sarcastic but re-states what he already said. Paul received his gospel from God; he did not require the approval of men to validate it. These leaders—which included Peter, John, and James—did not change Paul's gospel to the Gentiles, just as he did not change their gospel to the Jews.[31] Their messages were the same, although each party addressed a different ethnic group. The leaders in Jerusalem "recognized the grace" God had given to Paul (i.e., the ministry with which God had commissioned him); Paul was not in competition with them, but they considered each other as equals.

This is the essential point that Paul wants to communicate to the Galatians—in essence, "You keep hearing that I am not preaching the entire gospel, yet I am preaching the *same* gospel that is being preached in Jerusalem!" The "pillars" reference is consistent with what Paul has said elsewhere (as in 1 Cor. 3:11): these men built upon the foundation of Jesus Christ and supported His church with their own individual ministries.[32] These men extended to Paul and Barnabas "the right hand of fellowship"—

---

30 See Paul's reference to the "false circumcision," for example, in Phil. 3:2–3.

31 Four of these men—Paul, Peter, John, and James—are responsible for 21 of the 27 books of the NT. To see them in full agreement here is yet another testament to the unity of Christ's gospel.

32 Obviously, these ministries were not exclusively devoted to one group or the other: Peter preached to Gentiles (such as Cornelius and company); Paul preached to Jews; and John foresaw Christ's concern for both (John 10:16, 12:32). Yet the predominance of each man's efforts did focus on one particular group.

much more than a mere handshake, this act symbolized full acceptance of the missionaries and pledged support for future endeavors as well. "They only asked us to remember the poor" (2:10)—likely, the poor in Jerusalem. This was the only request made by Paul, even though he was already in agreement with it (see Acts 20:35, 2 Cor. 8:9–15, etc.).

Paul's Confrontation with Peter (Gal. 2:11–21)

At some point after Paul's visit to Jerusalem, Peter (Cephas) made a visit to Antioch—no doubt to investigate for himself the news he had heard concerning Paul and Barnabas' work there (2:11). When he first arrived, Peter moved freely among the Gentile converts and ate with them—a sign of acceptance and solidarity. When men from Jerusalem arrived, however, Peter changed his practices and his attitude; he withdrew from the Gentiles, making a distinction between himself (a Jew) and them (2:12).[33] These "certain men from James" did not accurately represent James himself (see Acts 15:24) but did closely identify with him. The "party of the circumcision" indicates their Jewish prejudices toward Gentile converts. They also were intimidating, convincing Peter, Barnabas, and other Jewish believers to embrace their partiality. "The worst feature of this [fearful] action was the evil effect it produced at Antioch. Why did Peter not fear that? He thought only of himself and of possible attacks from already completely discredited Judaizers."[34]

Paul's Rebuke of Peter (2:14–21): Paul understood the seriousness of this situation immediately. These men were "not straightforward about the truth of the gospel" (2:14a)—i.e., they were acting hypocritically, and thus violated the unity of the church and their own principles (Acts 15:7–10). Paul thus confronted Peter (and possibly others) publicly.[35] Peter was in sin

---

33 No doubt these Jews separated themselves from the Gentiles not only because of racial differences, but also dietary differences. The Jewish purist thought it wicked to eat with a Gentile; but he also considered the Gentiles' foods and manners (i.e., failing to wash ceremoniously) contemptible.

34 Lenski, *Interpretation*, 97; bracketed word is mine.

35 "Picture the scene; it was surely dramatic in the highest degree. We know of no other case after Pentecost when one apostle corrected another. The aorist [i.e., the completed-action tense of the verb "withstood"—MY WORDS] is significant and implies that Paul

and—as a leader of the church—this had to be dealt with before all those against whom he had sinned. The reasons why Paul would include this scenario in his letter to the Galatians include:

- Paul's apostolic authority was not in any way inferior to that of Peter.
- Paul showed no partiality toward Jews, Gentiles, or even fellow apostles.[36]
- The Judaizers had accused Paul (to the Galatians) that he was preaching an incomplete gospel; Paul demonstrates that it is the Judaizers themselves who misrepresented the gospel for their own gain.
- Legalism leads to separatism, and partiality leads to hypocrisy; neither legalism nor partiality has anything to do with the gospel of Christ (Eph. 2:8–9, Rom. 2:9–11).[37]
- The Judaizers pretended that their Jewish ethnicity made them superior people (or, closer to God), when in fact all have sinned against God, all need to be redeemed by the same Savior, and all must submit to the same gospel.
- The Judaizers sought conformity among men, not righteousness before God; this fact exposed their self-serving agenda (see 6:12–13).
- Since Peter was in sin, he needed to be confronted with a view toward restoration, which is exactly what Paul will teach in 6:1–2.
- From this scenario, it was evident that Paul taught a uniform, consistent,

---

withstood successfully, that Peter had no defense, that he yielded. Think how this smashed the Judaistic contention which would have Peter correct Paul and never Paul correct the great Peter" (*ibid.*, 92). Robertson takes it further: "One is a bit curious to know what those who consider Peter the first pope will do with this open rebuke by Paul, who was in no sense afraid of Peter or of all the rest" (*Word Pictures*, 288).

36 "The controversy with Cephas [Peter] revealed two aspects of Paul's character: his willingness to accept responsible leadership in a time of controversy and uncertainty, and his personal detestation of any kind of compromise in action" (Tenney, *Galatians*, 82).

37 "While legalism is not a Bible word, it defines a Bible subject. ... Legalism is the 'boot-strap' method of self-effort that places trust in mere human flesh to keep enough commandments to outweigh our sins. ... By its nature, legalism manifests itself in two forms—arrogance and fear. Those who trust in themselves that by their works they are righteous set themselves as a standard against which others are measured. This is why Jesus said they 'viewed others with contempt' (Luke 18:9–14). Legalism also nourishes the insidious fear of conscientious and obedient but misinformed Christians that they simply cannot know if they have done enough to be saved. In despair some reign themselves to the gnawing sickness of the uncertainty of their eternal future. ... Legalism makes question marks rather than exclamation points" (Wharton, *Freed for Freedom*, 27–28).

and accurate gospel that did not cater to persuasions of men or religious politics.

Paul presents an irrefutable case against the Judaizers—and against Peter specifically (2:14b–21). (It is unclear from the original Greek text whether his comments after 2:14 were actually spoken to Peter or are simply Paul's further exposition on what was said at the time.[38])

- **First,** Paul points out the obvious: when Peter is with Gentiles, he lives like a Gentile; when he is with Jews, he compels Gentiles to live like Jews (2:14b).
- **Second,** Paul admits that Jews have had better opportunity than the Gentiles ("sinners") until now, but that *no* man can justify himself before God based upon his works (i.e., human effort, as demonstrated through law-keeping) (2:15–16).
- **Third,** Christ will justify no one who engages in sin—in this case, the sin of hypocrisy and partiality. By rebuilding the very wall (or barrier) that Christ tore down through His redemptive work on the cross (see Eph. 2:13–16), Peter and the others transgressed His gospel. Put another way: if both Jews *and* Gentiles are sinners—and are both redeemed by the same means—there is no justifiable reason for their separation. In effect, "We were sinners already despite being Jews. Christ simply revealed to us our sin."[39] Christ is not a minister of sin, and neither can those be who minister to Him (2:17–18).[40]
- **Fourth,** Paul strenuously upholds the *exclusive allegiance* of the Christian: one who lives to Christ can no longer live by any other person; one who is justified by Christ cannot be justified by any other means (2:19–20). To "die to the Law" means to be under its

---

38 Conybeare and Howson, for example, believe that Paul's words to Peter end in 2:16 (*Life and Epistles*, 483).

39 Robertson, *Word Pictures*, 289.

40 Some commentators believe that Paul implies an argument against "antinomianism" [lit., against (or without) law], a fear among Jewish legalists that by leaving behind the constructs of the Law, men would be "free" to sin without consequence. Thus, to a Judaist, "living by faith" sounded like "living without the structure or constraint of law." (Paul argues against this more directly in Rom. 6.) This may be another explanation behind his statement, "Is Christ a minister of sin? May it never be!" (JFB, *Commentary* [electronic], on 2:17).

commandments and constraints no longer; "No master is able to give orders to a dead slave."[41] With these words, Paul makes clear the Christian's *complete legal separation* from the Law of Moses (or any man-made laws and impositions). "I have been crucified with Christ"—i.e., as real and effective as was His literal death, so is Paul's own "death" to all previous allegiances (see Rom. 6:3–11). Now he "[lives] by faith" rather than be justified by law; he no longer lives for (or to) himself, but Christ lives in him (see Rom. 1:17, 8:9).

- **Fifth,** the one who seeks to be justified by law-keeping after having been justified by Christ completely contradicts his need *for* Christ (2:21). If a person can be justified by his own effort, then there is no need for divine help and "Christ died needlessly."

This last thought introduces the entire next section of Paul's epistle. Lipscomb rightly observes, "Thus he has vindicated, without dispute, his apostleship, and that the law was dead, and that life and salvation are to be found through Christ, and he urges the folly of leaving the gospel, and turning to the Law of Moses or to any theory of man."[42] He will present the gospel as a message of unity and freedom, not a re-packaged Jewish law that continued to impose segregation and bondage upon non-Jewish converts.

---

41   Lenski, *Interpretation*, 114.
42   Lipscomb, *Commentary*, 217.

SECTION TWO:
SALVATION BY GRACE VERSUS JUSTIFIED BY LAW (3:1—4:31)

The True "Children of Abraham" (Gal. 3:1–14)

Paul Rebukes the Galatians (3:1–5): "You foolish Galatians, who has bewitched you?" (3:1). Paul depicts the Galatian Christians as having been charmed or (intellectually) seduced by the Judaizers and put under their spell. This was "foolish" because they ignored what Paul had originally taught them and so easily allowed these impostors to con them. In doing so, they devalued Christ's work on the cross and trusted instead in their works of law. Yet, Paul had so eloquently portrayed the crucified Christ that it was as if they had witnessed the event themselves.[43] "The vivid picture Paul had painted depicting the death of Christ before their eyes should have been enough to counteract all fascination."[44]

Paul then cuts to the heart of the problem: they did not receive the Spirit through works of law (or, human performance) upon their conversion. And they could not *maintain* fellowship with the Spirit through works of law, either. In other words, nothing has changed (3:2). Paul's teaching—as well as a fundamental understanding of the gospel of Christ—taught absolute dependence upon the grace of God for salvation. The Galatians had admitted and responded to this dependence when they were baptized into Christ; now they acted as if they no longer needed such help. "Having begun by the Spirit, are you now being perfected by the flesh?" (3:3)—or, as Lenski paraphrases, "Pray, what are you Galatians thinking to start in one way and to conclude in the exactly opposite way, to start in the right and most blessed

---

[43] This portrayal is not limited to the physical details of crucifixion, for this would likely already be known to the Galatians. More importantly, it refers to Christ's divine nature, His innocence, and the fact that He was entirely unworthy of execution—especially the lowliest of all executions.

[44] JFB, *Commentary* [electronic], on 3:1.

way and to end in the utterly wrong and ruinous way? This is not even sane thinking."[45]

The phrase "by the Spirit" (3:3) may refer to the fact that they Galatian Christians were able to perform miracles with His power (see 3:5),[46] but in a broader sense this necessarily involves the Spirit's work in one's conversion *and* the continuing fellowship that the believer enjoys in Christ (see John 3:5, Rom. 8:9, 14, Eph. 2:18, 3:16, etc.). In any case, one's justification does not rest upon the mere observance of laws but the grace of God. Paul asks wonderingly, "Did you suffer so many things in vain?" (3:4)—no doubt a reference to the initial trouble and opposition they endured upon the founding of their churches. The apostle fears that their spirit of legalism will undermine all the good that both he and they had already accomplished.

Paul Cites Abraham's Example (3:6–9): Paul draws a parallel between the Galatians' dependence upon God's Spirit and Abraham's own dependence upon God's having credited him with righteousness (3:6; see Gen. 15:6 and Rom. 4:1–5). Abraham is an ideal example to draw upon because from his lineage comes both Jews *and* Gentiles; thus, he is "our forefather according to the flesh" (Rom. 4:1). Furthermore, Abraham preceded the Law of Moses, which means that God's system of justification pre-dates that which the Judaizers promoted. Abraham needed to demonstrate his faith in God through works, but his *righteousness* (or justification) was determined by his faith (and not the works themselves) and was credited ("reckoned") to him by God. Thus, Paul implies that whatever a man receives from God regarding his salvation rests upon God's work, not that man's.

---

45 Lenski, *Interpretation*, 128. "The word *flesh* does not here mean sinful nature, but the power source to complete the Christian life. ... To walk by the flesh is to walk by faith in the power of one's own flesh to make himself acceptable to God" (Wharton, *Freed for Freedom*, 95).

46 It cannot be determined conclusively whether Paul here refers to the miracles that *they* performed, or those that *he* performed among them (which seems more likely). Either conclusion does not change his point, however: *no* miracle can be performed by human hands apart from the power of the Holy Spirit—a power that does not rest upon human effort.

Likewise, in the same way God credited Abraham with righteousness, so He credits Christians.[47] To be a "son of Abraham" in this context (3:7) means to be a partaker of that which God promised *to* Abraham. (The opposite is also true, as Jesus declared: to refuse to believe like Abraham separates one from the promises given to him; see John 8:39–40.) "Scripture" here is personified, having an intelligent and prophetic voice (3:8); indeed, the Holy Spirit is the inspiration and "voice" of the word of God. Thus, the Spirit—beginning with Abraham and continuing through Moses and the prophets—has long preached the coming gospel of *universal salvation* (see Gen. 12:3, 22:18). This promise (gospel) pre-dates the Law and has since been fulfilled in Christ (Eph. 3:1–12). One who shares Abraham's faith in God's ability to do what is humanly impossible—and salvation is humanly impossible!—also shares in the (spiritual) inheritance promised to him (3:9; see 3:29).

No One (But Christ) Is Justified by Law (3:10–14): The Law of Moses declared that everyone who does not keep that Law (perfectly) is under a curse (3:10; see Deut. 27:26 and James 2:10–11). The Judaizers failed either to communicate this or take it into account when they compelled Gentile believers to keep the Law. The Jews knew they could not keep the Law but wanted to make the Law a "yoke" or unbearable burden upon others (as Peter observed in Acts 15:10). Yet Paul points out the obvious: perfect obedience to law will earn one's righteousness; God condemns anything short of this. The transgressor of law can no longer depend upon his law-keeping to save him: he is now a lawbreaker. Righteousness is no longer something he has earned but is only something which God can grant (or credit) to him. Thus, "The righteous man shall live by faith" and not by his self-justification (3:11; see Rom. 1:17 and Heb. 10:37–39).

The fact that God has declared that man's righteousness comes through *faith* and not by *law* necessarily implies that all men are indeed *lawbreakers* (Rom. 3:19–23). Justification by Law—really, any "law"—is not a matter of faith but flawless obedience; a perfect law-keeper does not need to be justified by faith since because of his obedience he "will live" (Lev. 18:5). When Paul

---

47 The fact that Abraham was under a different covenantal system than are Christians does not negate the over-arching means by which God justifies *all* men: by the impartation of divine grace through the demonstration of human faith (Eph. 2:8).

says that "the Law is not of faith" (3:12), he means that the Law—really, any law given to men to obey—cannot rectify a law-breaker's condemnation. This is only possible through faith in God—something that law does not allow for.

The believer's hope lies not in his law-keeping but in the One who redeems him from condemnation (3:13). The lawbreaker is under a curse—a divine death sentence from which he cannot free himself either by human effort or any other means. Paul's point: one does not obtain righteousness through a mixture of Christ's effort (as when one became a Christian) and one's own law-keeping (after Christ has already redeemed him). His sole Deliverer is Christ; there is no other Redeemer. Human effort cannot remove divine condemnation; only divine intervention can do this. In effect, Christ has "become a curse for us"—*not*, "Christ was cursed instead of us" but (in essence) "Christ *satisfied* through His own offering what God requires of those who are cursed" (see Heb. 10:10).[48] God did not curse His own Son, but He did allow His Son to become a vicarious (substitutionary) sacrifice for those who are indeed under a curse (see 2 Cor. 5:21).[49] Christ *portrayed* or took on the *image* of a cursed man when He was hanged upon the cross—a type of "tree" (see Deut. 21:23).

By choosing to justify themselves by law, the Galatian Christians unwittingly incurred law's condemnation; by refusing Christ's justification (by their faith

---

[48] Wharton expresses what is probably on the minds of other Christians as well: "Jesus was literally cursed when He was crucified [citing Deut. 21:22ff]. Hence His cry from the cross, 'My God, My God, why hast thou forsaken Me?' God forsook Him that He might not have to forsake us" (*Freed for Freedom*, 103). I strongly disagree with this conclusion. First, Jesus took on the *role* of one cursed, which is far different from being the *object* of a curse. Second, it is a long-standing tradition that God literally "forsook" His Son. Jesus' words on the cross (Mat. 27:46) are from Psalm 22, which—if one reads the entire psalm—does not conclude that God *did* forsake the psalmist (David) but that he felt as miserable as one who *was* forsaken by Him. This is exactly how Jesus uses the same expression: bearing the sins of the world upon Himself felt like being all alone without God. Third, the very idea that God forsook His beloved Son under *any condition* jars violently against the rest of Scripture, including Jesus' own words (John 16:32). This idea that God abandoned at the cross is based on speculation and tradition, not biblical teaching.

[49] This cursed status applied to Gentiles as well as Jews. The Jews failed to keep their own Law, and therefore were condemned by that Law; but the Gentile also failed to keep whatever law he lived under, and thus was condemned by his lawlessness. This is the argument Paul makes in Rom. 2:5–16.

in His ability to do for them what they could not do for themselves), they rejected all avenues of grace—as Paul will plainly state later in this epistle. The Galatians could not receive the blessing that God promised to Abraham through their own work but only through Christ's redemptive work on the cross. Likewise, one does not receive the promise of the Spirit—not only the reception of the Spirit Himself but also all the blessings associated with His presence—by law-keeping but only by faith (3:14). As Paul is about to argue in the next section, divine promises are not dependent upon human effort but divine action. No person can duplicate God's power; no person can replace the effects of divine grace with his own self-righteousness. Only Jesus—who was God in the flesh—was able to overcome the limitations of the human condition.

The Purpose of the Law (Gal. 3:15–29)

Paul now directs the Galatians' attention to the fact that God's promise to (or covenant with) Abraham did not rest upon human effort but divine intervention (3:15). If the terms of a covenant agreement between two men are unalterable, then certainly the provisions of God's covenant with (a) man are unalterable and immutable. Men could not change the covenant God made with Abraham, nor did its fulfillment rest upon the work of men (i.e., law-keeping). Paul argues in this section that Christ was the fulfillment of that covenant—He is the unique and singular "seed" of promise (3:16; see Gen. 3:15 and 22:16–18). If Christ fulfilled the promise to Abraham, it could not have been fulfilled *before* Him or by anyone *but* Him. Thus, neither the Law of Moses *nor* the Israelite nation fulfilled the promise of universal salvation through the "seed" of Abraham. Furthermore, the Law could not change what God had promised. He did not alter His covenant with Abraham to accommodate the Law of Moses; in fact, this first covenant is *greater* than the Law itself (3:17).[50] Laws given to men never replace heaven's divine grace. If the Law was the fulfillment of God's promise to Abraham, then universal salvation would rest upon the work of men rather than God—rendering salvation impossible (3:18).

---

50 The "four hundred and thirty years" (roughly) represents the time between God's reaffirmation of His promise to Abraham (Gen. 15:13) and the giving of the Law at Sinai (Exod. 19).

The Law and the Promise (3:19–22): If the Law did not fulfill or change the promise of God, the natural question would be: "What, then, was the purpose *of* the Law?" (3:19). Paul's initial response: "It was added because of transgressions"—i.e., the Law magnified the need for this universal salvation by proving (over the course of 1,500 years) that *people are unable to save themselves* through their own efforts. God's having provided Israel with His expectations for perfect behavior only magnified how *imperfect* the Israelites really were. Put another way: God's holy law revealed not only His divine holiness but also man's carnal *unholiness*. The Law did not bring men into fellowship with God but in fact separated men further from Him; the Law could not redeem a single sin because only the grace of God can redeem sins—a divine action that transcends mere commandments given to men.

This Law, nonetheless, originated in heaven; it was ordained (or given) through angels (Acts 7:53 and Heb. 2:2–3). The "mediator" here (3:19) is Moses: God was represented by His angels; Moses represented the Israelites. "Now ... God is {only} one" (3:20)—i.e., when the "seed" would come, God would not speak through a third-party mediation but directly.[51] Indeed, the gospel of Christ was neither delivered by angels nor mediated through a human representative but was spoken to men by God in person—"in the flesh" (John 1:14, 1 Tim. 2:4–5, and Heb. 1:1–2).

The Law was weak (as in *limited* and *temporary*) in comparison to the promise (the "seed"). It was not contrary to God's promises, but it was not the fulfillment of them, either. The Law was only for men; it could not replace what God alone can do. Law cannot impart life to the sinner but can only assign a death sentence. If it *could* impart life, there would be no need for Christ or His gospel: righteousness would be based entirely upon human performance (3:21). As it is, "the Scripture has shut up [or, imprisoned] everyone under sin" (3:22)—i.e., through divine commandments given to men, God proved for the last time that law is not the route to human salvation. It is "as if the lid closed in on us over a massive chest that we could not open."[52] What people need, then, is not more law but *divine grace*. This

---

51 The problem with a third-party intermediary is that this person lacks independent authority; he is merely a spokesman from the one party to the other. Thus, Moses, as great as he was in the eyes of the Jews, could not compare to Christ, who spoke from His own divine authority (Heb. 3:1–6).
52 Robertson, *Word Pictures*, 297. Lenski (*Interpretation*, 175–176) notes that Scripture

grace comes "by faith in Jesus Christ" rather than works of law. "The fact that men are all prisoners to sin contrasts with the fact that Christ has made all men free."[53]

The Law of Moses and the gospel of Christ were never in competition, however. Taken together, they provide us with a rich understanding of both sin *and* salvation. The Law defined sin and yet anticipated a perfect sacrifice for sin; the gospel defines grace and mercy yet appeals to the Law to justify Christ's worthiness. The Law makes a man a sinner, so to speak, in that it reveals his utter sinfulness (see Rom. 7:7–12). But grace makes a sinner a saint through the perfect life of One (Christ) who was justified by law. Law (by itself) does not transform men into holy servants of God. Grace *does* change men—indeed, it always has—but grace never operates in the absence of human faith.

> The function of the law was preparatory and temporary. God never intended it to be His final method of saving men; indeed, the very sacrifices stipulated by the law were an admission of its imperfection, for they would not have been necessary had man been able to keep the law perfectly by his own unaided strength. On the other hand, the law was a revelation of God's inflexible holiness that requires man to meet His standards if man would know Him and enjoy eternal life. It was intended to act as a regulative and restraining influence upon human life between the promise of God and the fulfillment of that promise.[54]

The Law as a Tutor (3:23–25): Before God revealed the full message of salvation by faith *in Christ*, the Jews had been under the guardianship of the Law (or simply, "law") (3:23). Thus, Paul likens the Law to a "tutor" [Greek, *paedagogue*]—lit., "a guardian and guide of boys. Among Greeks and Romans, the name was applied to trustworthy slaves who were charged with the duty of supervising the life and morals of boys belonging to the better

---

does not shut up "everyone" but—in the literal reading of the Greek—"everything." That is, Scripture not only imprisons all men, without exception, but also everything *about* men—all of man's attempts to achieve and alleged demonstrations of self-righteousness.

53 JFB, *Commentary* (electronic), on 3:21.
54 Tenney, *Galatians*, 126.

class. The boys were not allowed so much as to step out of the house without them before arriving at the age of manhood."[55]

Law is not an end unto itself (3:24; see Rom. 10:2–4); "The Law of Moses served as a tutor to fit and train the Jewish people, or those who kept it, for Christ. This was the mission of the law."[56] "But now" (3:25)—i.e., *things have changed*, and they have changed permanently. God never goes backward but always forward; likewise, the Galatian Christians (and all Jewish Christians, for that matter) were never required to go *backward* to living under the Law but *forward* to living by faith.[57] Tutelage is no longer needed; the gospel of faith in Christ has been revealed to all men (Heb. 8:10–11).

Sons of God by Faith (3:26–29): "For you are all sons of God through faith in Christ Jesus" (3:26): the Christian's identity with God is not through law (or meritorious performance) but faith in Christ. Keeping the Law of Moses would not make a person *more* of a son of God than he already was; in fact, it would contradict his faith in Christ. The implication, too, is that Christians are no longer (spiritual) children but adults—therefore, they no longer need the Law to tutor them and are legally entitled to an inheritance.[58]

Baptism serves as the visible, historical marker of one's change of allegiance.[59] Since the Galatian Christians have been baptized *into* Christ, they belong to Him and Him alone—not to the Law, or the Judaizers, or even Paul (3:27). To "clothe" oneself with Christ means to surrender one's own identity to be identified solely with Christ (see Rom. 13:14).[60] This

---

55 Thayer, *Definitions* (G3807).

56 Lipscomb, *Commentary*, 234.

57 This is a major theme of *Hebrews*. I recommend my *Hebrews Commentary* for a fuller explanation of these thoughts; go to www.spiritbuilding.com/chad.

58 This is *not at all* to suggest that there is no longer any value in studying the Law of Moses, for that is untrue. The better we understand the Law and the prophets, the better we understand the gospel of Christ. Paul's emphasis does not address the value of studying, however, but the fact that the purpose *of* the Law has been fulfilled, and thus it is no longer binding. Furthermore, one cannot serve the Law *and* Christ simultaneously.

59 For a full study on "baptism," I strongly recommend my book, *Being Born of God: The Role and Significance of Baptism in Becoming a Christian* (Spiritbuilding Publishers, 2014); go to www.spiritbuilding.com/chad.

60 The meaning here is the same as what Jesus taught in (figuratively) eating His flesh and drinking His blood (John 6:54). Through such radical and irreversible action, the believer

"clothing" marks a permanent change of allegiance from one master (sin and condemnation) to another (Christ). The idea of being properly clothed to serve God also alludes to the special garments required of the Levitical priests (Exod. 28): one who was not properly clothed was unprepared to serve God. Thus, being clothed with Christ makes us equipped for every good work in service to God (Heb. 13:20–21, Rev. 3:17–18, etc.): it is to wear the King's clothes, so to speak. And if one is clothed with Christ, he does not need something *else* to be done to prepare him—such as putting himself under the yoke of the Law.

The pious Jew might have thought that he had to *lower* himself to the level of a Gentile "in Christ," yet Paul says just the opposite. It is "in Christ" that both Jew *and* Gentile are raised up to stand with God as was never possible. In this sense, all people—without reference to ethnicity, social status, or gender—are *equal* as brothers and sisters "in Christ" (3:28). (This does not mean earthly relationships, responsibilities, or gender roles are irrelevant. This equality regards our spiritual standing with Christ, not our earthly human relations.) "[Y]ou are all one"—which is exactly what had been predicted (Isa. 49:5–6, John 10:16) and what Christ had desired (John 17:20–22; see Eph. 2:13–16). This "oneness" defines the believers' *spiritual fellowship* with each other, which itself is based upon each person's spiritual union with Christ (1 Cor. 6:17).

What Paul declares here is unprecedented and revolutionary: never in all history have different ethnicities, different social classes, *and* different genders all been put *on an equal plane* in any context. This also strongly defies the Judaizers' attempt to keep such distinctions (and separations) alive by making themselves lords over and legal accountants of the Gentile believers. There is no partiality with God, whether regarding salvation or judgment (Rom. 2:9–11, 10:11–13); neither should there be partiality within the church (1 Cor. 11:17–22, 1 Tim. 5:21, James 2:1–4, 4:12, etc.). All those who belong to Christ are spiritual descendants of Abraham, since they manifest the same kind of faith that Abraham exhibited (3:29). Only these people are *true* sons of God and thus "heirs according to [the divine] promise"

---

internalizes Christ, or accepts His identity as His own. Thus, Paul said, "It is no longer I who live, but Christ lives in me" (Gal. 2:20).

(see Mat. 10:11–12). Those who attempt to justify themselves before God through their own means forfeit this promise, as Paul will go on to explain.

Paul's Personal Appeal to the Galatians (Gal. 4:1–20)

Waiting for the Promise (4:1–3): Paul now puts the Law of Moses and gospel of Christ in their rightful contexts. He begins his discussion with reference to Jewish Christians (4:1–5), but later includes Gentile believers as well. (Prior to the gospel, both groups were "held in bondage": the Jew to the Law of Moses; the Gentile to his pagan beliefs.) Just as a father determines the conditions of an inheritance and when it will be given, God determined the conditions and timing of the Jews' inheritance of the gospel. While blood relations often determine earthly inheritance, one's inheritance of the promises of God is dependent upon spiritual conditions and God's own sovereign decisions. While the Jews were under the tutelage of the Law, they could not receive the inheritance: they were not yet ready; the fullness of time had not yet come.

In a sense, the children of Israel were no different than the status of a house servant: they were both under the master's care and neither had received an inheritance (4:1–2). These "elemental things"—i.e., primary, rudimentary basics—do not refer specifically to the Law itself but "the earthly things with which the law had to do."[61] While under the Law, the Jews had limited understanding of their relationship with God; it was not until the Son revealed Himself could they see beyond this (4:3; see John 8:35–36).

Heirs of God through Christ (4:4–7): "But when the fullness of the time came" (4:4)—i.e., when all the *sequences* of events and necessary *conditions* had been met, Christ was sent into the world. "The Greek emphatically declares that God sent 'his own Son,' making a distinction between Christ, who is his own Son, and the believers, who are sons by adoption."[62] (Also, His having been "sent" necessarily implies a conscious pre-existence.) Jesus was "born of a woman" but without the involvement of a man: having been

---

61   Lenski, *Interpretation*, 196.
62   JFB, *Commentary* (electronic), on 4:4.

conceived in this manner, Jesus was both human *and* divine all at once.⁶³ This indicates God's divine action in fulfilling the promise to Abraham: the Savior's birth was not made possible by human effort but an act of God (Luke 1:31–35).

Jesus was also born "under the Law"—i.e., He was subject to all the Law's requirements, just as were His Jewish countrymen. This means that Jesus never came to *change* the Law but only to *fulfill* it (Mat. 5:17–19). If He had at any time violated the Law (by changing, defying, or ignoring it in any way), He could not have been obedient to it (Heb. 5:8–9). His obedience to God's laws was crucial to His being a worthy offering for sin; if He had disobeyed the Law at any time (even once—James 2:10), He would have become a *lawbreaker* rather than a law-*keeper*.⁶⁴ He could not have fulfilled the Law by having broken it but only by having kept it perfectly. It was necessary that the Law be *fulfilled* before God could bring that phase of His dealings with men to a close. Once Christ fulfilled the covenant God had made on Sinai, He could then introduce a new covenant, one not inaugurated with the blood of animals but with the blood of God (Mat. 26:27–28).

Through this new covenant (defined by the gospel), He could "redeem those who were under the Law" who stood condemned because of their sins against it (4:5). Through the only begotten Son of God, Jews could be legally adopted as spiritual sons of God by grace through faith. As "sons," they would thus be qualified to share in the inheritance God had provided for them (4:6; see Rom. 8:14–17 and Col. 1:12). "Abba" is an Aramaic word translated "daddy," yet Paul is not suggesting that believers address God in this way. He simply refers here to a term of intimacy and

---

63 "Born of" might be better translated "made to be of" or "became as one born of." "Such a translation would imply a previous state of existence (a thought most certainly in the context), whereas *born* does not" (E. Huxtable, *The Pulpit Commentary*, vol. 20 [Peabody, MS: Hendrickson Publishing, no date]), 183; see also Lenski's exposition (*Interpretation*, 199–202). It should be stated here, too, that "born of a woman" does not *definitively* allude to Christ's virgin birth, only to His having entered into a human existence.

64 Also consider Jesus' role as the King of Israel. The requirements for a king of Israel were spelled out in Deut. 17:14–20. One of those requirements was that he (the king) know and "carefully observing all the words of this law [i.e., the Law of Moses—MY WORDS] and these statutes." Those who think that Jesus came as a renegade crusader, out to change or reform the Law of Moses, contradict all that Moses, Jesus, and Paul said about Him.

familial endearment, made possible by the new relationship that believers have with the Father. This new relationship also provides for an otherwise unobtainable, otherworldly inheritance.

At this point, Paul no longer focuses solely on what God has offered to Jews but includes Gentiles as well (4:7). Both Jews and Gentiles—through the same process, for the same purpose, and by the same offering (Christ)—can become "sons" of God and thus heirs of His promises. Jewish believers are no longer slaves to the Law; Gentile believers are no longer slaves to paganism and idolatry. Just as God "sent" Jesus into the world to be its Redeemer, He sends "the Spirit of His Son" into the heart of each one who is redeemed.[65] Those who remain slaves will not receive any inheritance from the Father; only the sons are legally entitled to an inheritance (John 8:33-36). (Incidentally, the "sons" reference in *Galatians* always has reference to being qualified for a divine inheritance. It has nothing to do with gender, and thus is never meant to demean or exclude women.)

Losing Sight of the Big Picture (4:8–20): Paul now speaks directly to Gentile converts, since what he says here cannot describe the prior condition or mindset of the Jews (4:8-9). "[D]id not know God" is a phrase (or idea) he has used elsewhere to define the alienated state of godless Gentiles (Eph. 2:12, 4:18, 1 Thess. 4:5, and 2 Thess. 1:8). Immersed in paganism and idolatry, the Gentiles had previously enslaved themselves to unintelligent and powerless gods—fictitious entities which existed only in human imaginations. Yet while they were in their foolish and immature state, God called them into fellowship through His gospel: He had always known *them* but now He invited them to know *Him* as never before.[66]

---

65 "The Spirit of His Son" and the Holy Spirit are not two different "Spirits," but the same. The two expressions are interchangeable in Scripture (Rom. 8:9, 1 Peter 1:10–12). Once atoned of his sins by the blood of Christ, the believer is then sanctified (or sealed) by the Holy Spirit. Christ and the Spirit work in such seamless unity and cooperation that the Spirit of *God* also operates as the Spirit of *Christ*. Whoever belongs to Christ also belongs to the Father; his access to the Father is through the Spirit (Eph. 2:18).

66 As Rom. 1:18–23 explains, it was not as though the Gentiles had *never* known of God (or were *prevented* from knowing about Him), but that they deliberately chose to suppress that knowledge in pursuit of lesser things.

With such unprecedented hope and opportunity, Paul expresses his wonderment (and disappointment) at their enslavement to these lesser things all over again.[67] In this case, the commandments of *law* became a kind of "god" to which they give their allegiance rather than to a literal idol. The object of their enslavement had changed but not their enslavement to earthly power (4:9). "[W]eak and worthless elemental things [or, rudimentary principles]" contrasts the ineffective things of this world (regarding religion) and the noble spiritual truths revealed by God. Even Judaism was weak and worthless as a means of obtaining righteousness. In other words, the Galatian believers, in accepting the impositions of the Judaizers, were going backward, not forward. "You observe days" (4:10)—i.e., you have become meticulously concerned with *signs* rather than *substance*; you have chosen to observe ritual ceremony over the Christ who truly deserves your full attention. These "days," etc. most naturally refers to ceremonial observances of the Law rather than those of cultic religion; regardless, the result was the same. In view of their decisions, Paul wonders if he has wasted valuable time and effort with them: "I fear for you, that perhaps I have labored over you in vain" (4:11).

Having stated his grave concern over the direction they have chosen, Paul still appeals to them as brethren and recalls their first encounter (4:12–14). "[B]ecome as I am"—i.e., a free man in Christ; "for I also have become as you are"—i.e., as one who was without (the) Law (cf. 1 Cor. 9:19–23). No doubt many Jews considered Paul a traitor to his countrymen and Jewish heritage; in their eyes, it was as if he had *become* a Gentile. "You have done me no wrong," he explains, in having received him as a Jew who desired to share the gospel with Gentiles. Yet, this is what makes their having turned away from him so inexplicable: they accepted him when he was like *them* (i.e., putting himself on the same footing with them) but now they turn to others (i.e., Judaizers) who force the Galatians to be like *them*.

We are not certain as to what "bodily illness [or, condition]" Paul refers; he does not disclose it within this epistle.[68] It is possible that this is the "thorn

---

[67] "Paul is implying that the works of the law of Moses, which he labels as 'weak and worthless elemental things,' are as impotent and worthless to free us from our sins as the weak and worthless elements of pagan idolatry" (Wharton, *Freed for Freedom*, 137).

[68] It is possible that Paul refers to his having been stoned and left for dead in Lystra (Acts 14:19–21). Even though he survived the experience, no doubt the physical wounds of one

in the flesh" he mentions later in 2 Cor. 12:7. Whatever it was, the Galatians received him in his stricken state and listened to his gospel message.[69] It seems apparent that these people did not just tolerate Paul's sickly condition but also nursed him back to good health. Instead of treating him with less respect because of his illness, they gave him the highest respect—as though he were a messenger ("angel") of God, just as Christ Himself was sent by God.

Having re-connected with them on this level, Paul now asks the Galatians, in essence, "What happened?" (4:15–16). "[Y]ou would have plucked out your eyes" may be proverbial or hypothetical, not likely a literal reference to Paul's actual ailment. This has not stopped many commentators, however, from assuming a severe eye malady, perhaps due to Paul's road-to-Damascus experience (Acts 9:17–18). Regardless, Paul admits that the Galatians would have made difficult and personal sacrifices for him (and his message) at first; but now things have changed considerably. Instead of continuing to befriend Paul, they have pulled away from him; instead of staying true to the message of his gospel, they have accepted another message (as though it were) on par with that gospel. "Have I become your enemy?" (4:16)—i.e., Paul hints at their insincerity, if indeed they would refuse him simply because he confronted them with the truth of their situation. (People are often quick to say they "want the truth" but then are offended when they hear it. Case in point: the Jews repeatedly asked Jesus to tell them "plainly" whether He was the Christ [John 10:24]. When He finally did, they accused Him of blasphemy and condemned Him to death [Mat. 26:63–66].)

Having said this, Paul then reveals the Judaizers among them to be insincere and acting upon ulterior motives (4:17–18). (He elsewhere identifies Jews who oppose his apostolic authority and teaching as "false apostles, deceitful workers," and "disguising themselves as servants of righteousness"—2 Cor. 11:13, 15.) Paul admits that it is always nice to be sought out; even he sought out the Galatians. Yet these false teachers were not looking to help the Gentiles but to enslave them to their own methods. In shutting out

---

who had been stoned produced a sight (to the Galatians) that would have been difficult to look upon.

69 "The first time" in the Greek means "the first of two," implying that Paul had visited the Galatians at least twice before writing this epistle.

the Galatians to Paul and the other churches, the Judaizers would exert full control over them.[70] This reveals their true motive: it was arrogant domination, not genuine love or concern. In other words, Paul's gospel had not changed but the Judaizers had changed Paul's gospel; "Legalism had robbed them of the blessings of grace."[71]

In sharp contrast to the self-serving motives of the Judaizers, Paul regards the Galatians in a tender and maternal manner (4:19–20). "I am again in labor"—i.e., it is like I am starting all over again (in trying to produce Christ in you). The imagery Paul uses here is unusual but effective. While typically Paul speaks of the believer conforming to the image of Christ (Rom. 8:29, 12:1–2), it is also true that Christ is, in a spiritual sense, being formed (as one's personal conviction) within the heart of the believer. The "tone" of this letter is the result of his inability to be with them in person; otherwise, he might be able to reason with them in a more conversational manner. As it is, he remains "perplexed" about their fickle change of heart—literally, he is at a loss to explain what has happened.[72]

The Allegory of Two Women (Gal. 4:21–31)

To expose the illogic and inconsistency of the Judaizers' teachings, Paul provides an allegory (or, symbolic representation) of two women: Sarah and Hagar (4:21ff). His case begins with historical facts, but he applies it as a spiritual lesson. The Judaizers compelled Gentile believers to be bound to the impositions of the Law; yet this backward-moving mentality contradicted their own biblical history. ("They loved to employ subtle, mystical, allegorical interpretations of Scripture which were often contrary to what the Scripture actually said."[73]) In other words, Paul appeals to Scripture itself to vindicate his position *and* expose the error of these false teachers.

---

70 "The Judaizers were proselyters; they merely invaded the young churches that had already been founded in order to appropriate them for themselves. ... They zealously sought and affected their victims, courted them in every way, clung to them like leeches. The proselyters of today continue this type" (Lenski, *Interpretation*, 227).

71 Lehman Strauss, *Devotional Studies in Galatians and Ephesians* (Neptune, NJ: Loizeaux Bros., 1957), 63.

72 Robertson, *Word Pictures*, 306.

73 JFB, *Commentary* (electronic), on 4:21.

"The law" here does not refer to the Law of Moses but to the Pentateuch, all of which was "law" to the Israelites. (One should read Gen. 16 and 21:9–21 to become familiar with the illustrations Paul uses in this section.)

Sarah and Hagar (4:21–23): While God had promised Abraham a son to perpetuate the promise given to him (4:21–23; see Gen. 15:3–4), Abraham struggled with the logistics of this. He was an old man; his wife was barren *and* beyond child-bearing years. To provide her husband with an heir, Sarah (also known as Sarai) offered Hagar, her Egyptian handmaid, to Abraham as a concubine.[74] Hagar did bear a son (Ishmael) for Abraham, but this was "according to the flesh" (i.e., of natural means or human effort), not a son of divine promise. Following this, God explicitly promised that *Sarah herself* would bear a son (Gen. 18:1–19). This happened exactly as God had predicted and overcame all the humanly insurmountable barriers that had previously prevented it. Thus, Isaac was a son of divine promise and miraculous intervention. The Jews descended from Isaac; thus, the promise of universal salvation came through the Jewish lineage. Furthermore, Hagar represents the exertion of human effort, while Sarah represents (in her experience of bearing Isaac) the supra-human work of God.

The Two Covenants (4:24–31): Paul draws upon this actual, historical situation in an allegorical[75] (or metaphorical) manner: "These women are two covenants" (4:24).[76] This is illustrated as follows (4:24–31):

---

74 Sarah likely reasoned that since the Lord had closed her womb (Gen. 16:2), she was left to produce a son for her husband in whatever means was necessary. In ancient times, the inability to produce a child indicated some defect or failure on the part of the wife; barrenness was a symbol of social disgrace.

75 "Allegories are in words what hieroglyphics are in painting. … Allegories, parables, and metaphors abound in the writings of the East. Truth was more easily treasured up in this way, and could be better preserved and transmitted when it was connected with an interesting story" (Albert Barnes, *Barnes' Notes*, vol. 11 [Grand Rapids: Baker Books, 1987], 370). In a sense, parables turn pictures into real truths; allegories turn real truths (or real historical events) into pictures, for the purpose of better understanding the reality.

76 The Jews reckoned a son's ethnicity through the mother, not the father; thus, Timothy was a Jew (and needed to be circumcised), even though his father was a Greek (Acts 16:1–3). Likewise, Ishmael was considered an Egyptian (a foreigner to the promises of God) and Isaac was considered a natural son (a rightful heir to these promises).

Hagar ("the bondwoman")	Sarah ("the free woman")
Has no relation to Abraham, the recipient of God's promises.	Abraham's wife, and shares in the promises given to Abraham.
Represents natural human effort.	Represents divine effort.
Ishmael is not the child of promise.	Isaac is the child of promise.
Corresponds with Mount Sinai (physical law-keeping).	Corresponds with Mount Zion (justification by grace through faith).
Corresponds with old Jerusalem (the literal, physical city).	Corresponds with New Jerusalem (the spiritual, otherworldly "city")—the church of Christ on earth.
Represents bondage (to law).	Represents freedom (through grace).
Her children (Jews) are slaves to law.	Her children (Christians) are free.[77]
Her children boast in their heritage and ethnicity.	Her children are born of the Spirit, and boast in Christ (see 6:14).
Her children (Jews) persecute those born to Sarah (Christians).	Her children (Christians) are persecuted by those enslaved to law.
Her children (Jews) will be "cast out" (see Heb. 13:9–14).	Her children will remain in the house forever (see John 8:35).

Paul's case is airtight and unassailable. The rabbinical way he has presented this allegory imitates what the Judaizers are fond of doing but does not succumb to their errors of interpretation. Promises of God are not dependent upon human effort or human intervention; God's people, therefore, are justified not by works of law but by divine mercy and grace.

---

[77] The quote in 4:27 is from Isa. 54:1, a messianic prophecy that is fulfilled in God's having produced innumerable "children" through the born-again process of conversion to Christ.

Such people comprise the "New Jerusalem" (Heb. 12:22–24), the "city" of promise which is built without human hands (Heb. 11:13–16).[78] We can state Paul's point in the form of a rhetorical question: "Why would anyone choose to be *enslaved without hope* instead of being *free in Christ*?" This sets up the discussion to follow in the next chapter.

---

78 It is conspicuous that Paul refers to the New Jerusalem (a.k.a. Christ's church) as "our mother" (4:26)—a feminine designation. The Jews rendered their ethnicity through the lineage of the mother, which is why, for example, Timothy was circumcised as a Jew even though his father was a Greek (Acts 16:1–3). This feminine characteristic is also applied to Christ's church as His "bride" (Eph. 5:25–27, Rev. 19:7–8, and 21:2).

Section Three:
Led by the Spirit versus Living by the Flesh
(5:1—6:10)

Freedom is Found in Christ, Not in Law (Gal. 5:1-15)

A **Yoke of Slavery (5:1-4)**: The Judaizers preached that the route to righteousness—and thus freedom (from sin)—came through legalism. Paul has demonstrated the illogic of this argument in the previous chapters; now he cuts to the chase. "It was for freedom that Christ set us free" (5:1a): Christ did not die to perpetuate slavery or give men another *form* of slavery. He did not respond to man's inability to keep law (perfectly) by giving him *more law*. Instead, Christ died to make men free (see Luke 4:16-19, John 8:31-32, Acts 13:38-39, Rom. 6:22-23, 8:2, and Heb. 2:14-15). "Freedom" here does not mean excused from law or not under obligation to keep laws. It means freedom from the condemnation that law brings to the one who fails to keep it perfectly.

"Therefore"—because of this fact—"keep standing firm" (5:1b): the ability to "stand" is set against the *fallen* condition of man apart from divine mercy and grace (Rom. 3:23). No sinner can "stand" before God on his own; it is Christ who makes us stand and prepares us for our presentation before the Father (Rom. 5:1-2, Col. 1:21-22). To "stand firm" also implies a tenacious adherence to the sound doctrine which has Christ's apostles have preached (Eph. 6:11, 13, Phil. 1:27, 2 Tim. 1:13, 2 Peter 3:17-18, etc.). Rather than being freed from doctrine, the believer is made responsible for preserving it (Eph. 4:3). While striving to be obedient to God, the believer not to become enslaved to the opinions, teachings, or impositions of men (1 Cor. 7:23).

To "receive circumcision" implies that one embraces the entire Law of Moses (5:2).[79] To do so would represent an act of defiance against Christ's

---

79 "If salvation is by law, why should one be obliged to keep just *one* ceremonial commandment, or even two or three, and not the rest? If the pathway to salvation is thought to lie in that direction [then] one should travel it to the very end" (Hendriksen, NTC, 196,

redeeming sacrifice and unbelief in God's system of justification by faith. A person cannot be justified by works of law *and* divine grace all at once; he must choose one system over the other. Just as the New Jerusalem is not compatible with the Old Jerusalem, so justification by works is incompatible with justification by faith. Paul issues a challenge to the Galatians to choose finally what they are going to do. With full apostolic authority, he declares that choosing *law* over *grace* will be of "no benefit" to them: Christ cannot save people who will not depend upon (or, put faith in) His power to save them. In fact, if one accepts circumcision, he obligates himself to keep the entire Law of Moses *perfectly*; otherwise, his justification is completely ruined (5:3).[80] "You have been severed from Christ … you have fallen from grace" (5:4): self-justification results in alienation from Christ and forfeits divine help.[81] Salvation that entirely depends upon human effort will inevitably fail. Paul's language here confirms the *fallibility* of the believer—i.e., Christians are not "once saved, always saved," as Calvinism assumes, but can indeed lose their salvation. One cannot be "severed" from something to which he was never connected; likewise, he cannot "fall" from a status which he never really had (cf. Heb. 10:26–31).

The Hope of Righteousness (5:5–6): Those who seek righteousness through legalism give up all hope in Christ. Those sanctified by the Holy Spirit, however, anticipate "the hope of righteousness" (5:5)—i.e., one's future redemption based on God's righteousness which He has always demonstrated (Rom. 1:16–17). One who puts full confidence in God's

---

bracketed word added). The act of circumcision served as a "sign of the covenant" with the children of Abraham (Gen. 17:7–14). The Jews' fixation on circumcision was undermined by the fact that God credited Abraham with righteousness *before* he was circumcised (Rom. 4:9–13). Besides this, the sign was not an end, but pointed forward to its fulfillment (or substance), which is Christ (Rom. 10:2–4, Col. 2:16–17, Heb. 10:1–10, etc.). Thus, by clinging to the sign rather than the substance actually showed great contempt toward God rather than serving to honor Him.

80 Someone might cite here the instance of Paul circumcising Timothy (Acts 16:1–3) as a contradiction to what he is saying here in *Galatians*. Yet, the two contexts are very different. Paul circumcised Timothy so that his *un*-circumcision would not interfere with his work among the Jews (since they knew he was a Jew, traced through his mother's lineage). In *Galatians*, Paul speaks of one who is being circumcised as a matter of *righteousness*, as a work of self-justification.

81 In my opinion: Paul intentionally uses the phrase "severed from Christ" regarding the practice of circumcision. In severing (or cutting off) the foreskin as a means of seeking righteousness, one severs himself from Christ.

ability to save him no longer rests upon his own works or merit but in God's mercy and grace. One's walk with Christ is defined not by legalism, symbolic actions (such as circumcision), or human performance but "faith working through love."[82] This *kind* of faith is "working"—it needs to be demonstrated by visible action—but is motivated by the love God demonstrated through the offering of Christ (1 John 4:9–10). Instead of imposing legalism and man-made teachings upon one another, Christians are to express their faith in God through their *service* to those who are in Christ. "A faith that works by love leads one to do the will of God, and to do good to his fellow men."[83] The legalists assumed that living by faith would lead to a failure to observe law; on the contrary, faith cannot be demonstrated without a qualified standard by which to define it; law provides this standard (Rom. 3:31). Faith cannot "work" without a defining standard or legal point of reference; it has no definition apart from actions (*of* faith) which makes it real and measurable (James 2:14–26).

Those Misleading the Galatians (5:7–12): Again, Paul addresses his virtual disbelief that the Galatians have so easily succumbed to the words of those who preached a different gospel than what he had preached. "You were running well; who hindered you?" (5:7)—lit., who cut into your path?[84] Paul had set the Galatians upon the path of fellowship with Christ and life with God; the Judaizers sought to divert their course to an entirely different direction. It was not God who diverted them from the path but those who had relatively little concern for their spiritual well-being (5:8).

"A little leaven" (5:9)—"leaven" is a common metaphor for illicit teaching, uncleanness, or any corruptive influence (Mat. 16:6, 1 Cor. 5:6). In other words, it takes only a small amount of error to corrupt a great amount of sound doctrine. A great amount of dough never turns a small amount of

---

82 Compare Paul's three "neither circumcision nor uncircumcision" statements: 1 Cor. 7:19, Gal. 5:6, and 6:15. In each case, he stresses what is *beneficial* as well as what is entirely useless (regarding salvation) (James Coffman, *Commentary on Galatians, Ephesians, Philippians, Colossians* [Austin, TX: Firm Foundation, 1977], 90).

83 Lipscomb, *Commentary*, 260. "Legalism is a lie. It affirms the impossible; it offers a system that condemns sinners as a system of salvation for sinners!" (Wharton, *Freed for Freedom*, 166).

84 "Hinder" means to beat or drive back; to hamper, shackle, or impede (Thayer, *Definitions* [electronic]; G1465).

yeast into dough, but a small amount of yeast will permeate the entire batch of dough.

The Galatians' about-face is exasperating to Paul: after spending so much time and effort teaching them—and risking his own life to do so (Acts 14:19)—a few false teachers infiltrate the group and hijack the congregations with smooth words and manipulative persuasion. Despite the damage that has been done, Paul has not given up on the Galatians (5:10). Yet he in effect places a curse upon the one(s) leading them astray (recall 1:8). It is one thing to be led astray because of one's own immature spiritual disposition; it is another thing to make oneself a stumbling block to such people.

Paul then makes a rhetorical argument: if he "preached circumcision"—i.e., if he supported the act itself in any way—then there would be no reason for the Judaizers' attacks against his character and authority (5:11). He is no doubt referring to his having had Timothy (and possibly others) circumcised to avoid being a stumbling block to Jews (Acts 16:1–3). His point: it is not *circumcision itself* that is the real point of contention but *the cross of Christ*. The Judaizers relied upon human works based upon legal requirements; the cross removed all such dependence and took away the boast of the pious, legalistic Jew. Christ, as they saw it, spoke against their love for laws; He minimized the importance of Moses and therefore was a threat to their entire belief system and way of life (John 9:27–29, Acts 21:20–22, etc.). He (Christ) did not allow for any means of justification other than *faith in Him*—and this underlying contempt for the gospel of Christ compelled the Judaizers to mix one teaching with the other.[85] Thus, Paul exposes their real motive and condemns it. "I wish that [they] would even mutilate themselves" (5:12)—lit., castrate themselves. There are several implications of this statement:

- ❏ Emasculation (or castration) was the practice of some pagan priests (of Cybele, for example), yet it profited them nothing. Likewise, even a severe "cutting off" of the flesh would not help the Judaizers (or anyone else) anymore than would mere circumcision.
- ❏ In the Law of Moses, an emasculated man could not enter the holy assembly (or convocation) of Israel or the court of the tabernacle. His

---

85 JFB, *Commentary* (electronic), on 5:11.

emasculation made him (physically) incomplete, and therefore unable to perform direct service to the Lord (Deut. 23:1; see Lev. 21:16–22, in principle).

- ❏ The "cutting off" may also refer to excommunication—in this case, not from the assemblies of Israel, but from the churches of Christ. Thus, Paul may be implying that these men were not fit for the Law *or* Christ, as they were insincere, self-serving, and under condemnation from God.

Freedom to Serve One Another (5:13–15): The Judaizers sought to enslave their converts; Christ calls people to freedom (5:13). This freedom refers to one's escape from divine condemnation; it does *not* refer to the freedom to do or teach whatever one chooses (see 1 Peter 2:16). No one has the freedom, for example, to teach a different gospel; accept a doctrine that did not come from God; make himself a stumbling block to others; enslave others with one's personal beliefs; indulge in sensual practices that corrupt the soul; etc.

At this point, Paul turns a corner in his discourse with the Galatians. He is no longer talking exclusively about Judaism and legalism but draws attention to the moral conduct of the Galatians themselves. (This will become more evident by the end of this chapter.) Even in Jesus' day, the Jews prided themselves on being meticulously observant to every technical commandment of the Law, yet they indulged in moral crimes and exploited every (alleged) legal loophole to their own advantage (Mat. 5:27–45, 22:23, Mark 7:9–13, etc.).[86] Paul warns the Galatians against both abuses: legalism itself *and* the license to behave badly when such behavior was not explicitly forbidden by a codified legal statement. Serving the "flesh"—whether one's human pride, quest for power (or control), or sensual pleasures—is incompatible with serving one another "through love." A person cannot pursue both directions and engage in both practices at the same time.

"For the whole Law is fulfilled in one word [lit., commandment], in the statement, 'You shall love your neighbor as yourself'" (5:14). In a sense, Paul turns the Judaizers' position on its head, as if to say, "If you *really* want to keep the Law, then *love your neighbor* in a godly manner, because this will fulfill all that the Law stood for" (see Mat. 22:37–40, Luke 10:25–28,

---

86 See Paul's further exposition on this thought in Rom. 2:17–24.

Rom. 13:8–10, and James 2:8). Since this is a *moral* commandment and not merely a ceremonial one (as circumcision was), it is a necessary part of *every* covenantal agreement that God makes with men. Whoever is in covenant with God—and thus obeys the laws required to honor that covenant—must love his "neighbor" as himself.

Legalism never produces a loving heart or a spirit of forbearance; no matter how innocently it begins, it always descends into a struggle for power, control, domination, and self-vindication. Legalism always pits one man's righteousness against another's; it separates and polarizes rather than reconciles and unites. It leads to biting, devouring, and the "consuming" (or destroying) of one another (5:15). The gospel of Christ, on the other hand, promotes love, peace, unity, acceptance, forbearance, and the fruit of the Spirit. Paul leaves the Galatians to decide which path to take but lays out the consequences of choosing anything other than the way of Christ (John 14:6).

Contrast of the Two Lifestyles (Gal. 5:16–26)

Walk by the Spirit (5:16–18): "For as a man thinks within himself, so he is" (Prov. 23:7). Whatever guides one's *heart* also guides his *lifestyle* (or behavior). Thus, the kind of visible behavior a person exhibits exposes—for better or worse—his heart. A heart led by the Holy Spirit produces "fruit of the Spirit"; a heart led by human pride and sensual appetites produces "deeds of the flesh." "[W]alk by the Spirit" (5:16) refers to a lifestyle conditioned by the Spirit-led attitude of one's heart. It does not merely mean, "Learn about spiritual things," "Act like a spiritual person," or "Experience the Spirit in your own subjective way." Such superficial interpretations fail to comprehend the essence of Paul's instruction. Paul refers to a full submission of one's own will to God's will; he speaks of allowing Christ to dominate one's heart (recall 2:20). One's heart that focuses upon the will of God and the Spirit of Christ will naturally diminish and properly subdue his desire for human pleasure and sensual gratification.[87]

---

87 "The spirit and the flesh mutually exclude one another. It is promised, not that we should have no evil lusts, but that we should 'not fulfil' them. If the spirit that is in us can be

The Spirit is pure and holy; the carnal man is corrupted with sin and self-ambition. These two "wills" have diametrically opposed objectives; they are entirely incompatible; coexistence is impossible (5:17). "[T]he things that you please" refers to practices born of carnal human lusts (or appetites); it does not mean that there is nothing pleasurable in serving Christ. Following the Spirit does what God wants; following our own lusts and appetites leads us to do what *we* want (but stands opposed to God). "But if you are led by the Spirit, you are not under the Law" (5:18)—or simply, "under law" (following the literal Greek text). One who is led by God is also justified by Him; one who is "under law" cannot be justified since he is a lawbreaker, and no amount of law-*keeping* will absolve him. Law magnifies sin (and thus shows the desperate need for grace) but cannot remove it (1 Tim. 1:8–11). Grace does not nullify the need for law, but it does what law cannot do: justify the sinner (Rom. 6:14–15).

The Deeds of the Flesh (5:19–21): "Now the deeds of the flesh are evident" (5:19)—i.e., of a public nature; they visible in the lives of unconverted people. A person *not* led by the Spirit will produce worldly and even satanic behavior. Paul mentions four basic groups of these deeds: sins of sensuality; sins of idolatry (including sorcery); sins of personal relations; and sins of drunkenness or similar excesses. Specifically, these are:

- **Immorality.** Technically, anything that is not *moral* (or, consistent with the nature or character of God) is *immoral*; the English word has broad application. But the Greek here [*porneia*, from which we get "pornography"] has reference to illicit sexual activity (adultery, fornication, homosexuality, bestiality, prostitution, etc.).[88] Such deeds are works of the flesh; they are not from God and are inconsistent with His divine nature (1 Thess. 4:2–8).
- **Impurity.** This refers to any moral uncleanness or indecency. The context can be physical, mental, or spiritual; it can be physically inappropriate behavior, a "dirty" mind, or any illegitimate worship of God.
- **Sensuality (or lasciviousness).** "Sensual" refers to the human senses

---

at ease under sin, it is not a spirit that comes from the Holy Spirit. The gentle dove trembles at the sight even of a hawk's feather" (JFB, *Commentary* [electronic], on 5:16).

88 Thayer, *Definitions* (electronic); G4202.

(or passions); correspondingly, this word refers to unrestrained human lust, desire, or behavior. This often implies a sexual context, but it can apply to other contexts as well. It includes indiscretion, shamelessness, debauchery, or any moral deficiency.

- ☐ **Idolatry.** The Greek word here [*eidololatreia*] translates to "image worship"; more generally, idolatry is any worship of anything other than God. This includes self-exaltation, creature worship, greed, covetousness, and pornography (Rom. 1:21–25, Eph. 5:5, Col. 3:5, and 1 John 2:15–16).
- ☐ **Sorcery (or witchcraft).** Sorcery, witchcraft, divination, and all forms of seeking power from demons or the dead, has long been condemned by God (Exod. 22:18, Lev. 19:31, 20:6, 26, Deut. 18:10, 11, 14, 2 Kings 21:6, etc.). Technically, the Greek word here [*pharmakeia*] is derived from a root word referring to a drug, potion, poison, or medication; our modern word "pharmacy" comes from this.[89] In ancient times, drugs (especially hallucinogens) were often used in conjunction with the magical arts, and especially the speaking of oracles or (allegedly) divine prophecies. (Either the "prophet" would be under the influence of drugs, or his listeners, or both.) More generally, the word here refers to any appeal to a (spiritual) power other than God to foresee the future, interpret signs, or influence an audience.
- ☐ **Enmities (or hatred).** Hatred is not always an evil thing; Christ "hates" (or, has hatred toward) anything that stands opposed to Him (Phil. 3:18, James 4:4, and Rev. 2:6, for example). In this case, however, Paul refers to a human hatred (or animosity) that is based upon evil or satanic motives (Titus 3:3). Those who are "haters of God" also make themselves enemies of God (and the word "enmity" comes from an old English-French word meaning "enemy") (Rom. 1:30, 2 Tim. 3:3). One cannot practice satanic hatred—especially toward a fellow believer—while claiming to love God (1 John 4:20).
- ☐ **Strife.** Christ's church has no room for factions, divisions, or rivalries; "strife" (or, contention) is often what causes such separations (1 Cor. 1:10, 3:3, 11:17–19, etc.). This includes any wrangling or debating (over words, opinions, or issues) that serves personal agendas (2 Tim. 2:14 and Titus 1:10–14) rather than seeking to contend earnestly for the faith (Jude 1:3).

---

89 Hendriksen, *NTC*, 219–20.

- **Jealousy.** Literally, the Greek word here [*zeloo*] means "to burn with zeal," "desire earnestly," or "to boil with envy, hatred, [or] anger."[90] In a positive sense, it refers to righteous zeal (2 Cor. 11:2); negatively, it refers to an ungodly appetite or passion for something that does not belong to a person, something threatened by another person, or the wicked passion itself. God wants us to be zealous and passionate about our faith in Him; however, He will not condone *self-serving* zeal (or, passion for that which is evil), which is what Paul has in mind here.
- **Outbursts of anger.** The KJV has "murder" here, which is too restrictive of a translation of the Greek word [*thumos*]. A better translation is fierce passion, explosions of wrath, or unbridled indignation, which "outbursts of anger" conveys. Certainly, murder can be a natural outcome of such outbursts (as in Acts 7:54–60); but this is not always the case. The main idea here is that of the absence of self-control while being overwhelmed by one's emotions.
- **Disputes.** While the idea here is similar to "strife" (that leads to factions and divisions), the Greek word [*eritheia*] involves self-promotion, as in jockeying for position to gain a better advantage (over someone else).[91] Thus, it implies a disingenuousness or insincerity in what is being discussed: one person is trying to come out ahead in an argument at his opponent's expense. Such arguments are unprofitable and contradict the tolerant and conciliatory attitude expected of God's people.
- **Dissensions and factions.** Having itemized the various ungodly *attitudes* that lead to factions, Paul now mentions the actual act of separation itself. "Factions" is translated from *hairesis*, from which we get "heresy."[92] It refers to a choice (or opinion) that departs from the main body of thought, as a religious party or sect (see 2 Peter 2:1). (Interestingly, the Jews considered Christianity itself to be a heresy or "sect"; see Acts 24:14.)
- **Envying.** Simply put, "envy" is a satanic spirit of jealousy mixed with ill-will directed at someone who has what the envier wants. It was "because of envy" that the Jews had delivered Jesus to Pilate (Mat. 27:18); some preachers also spoke against Paul because of envy (Phil. 1:15).

---

90 Thayer, *Definitions* (electronic); G2206.
91 *Ibid.*, G2052.
92 *Ibid.*, G139.

- **Drunkenness.** Drunkenness is hardly a first-century problem; ever since men learned to distill alcohol, this vice has plagued humankind. It is not the drink itself that Paul condemns here, but the over-indulgence of it. Drunkenness (or intoxication) breaks down inhibitions, but also incapacitates a person physically, mentally, and spiritually (1 Cor. 6:10, Eph. 5:18). Those who serve the Lord are prohibited from drunkenness (see Lev. 10:8–11, 1 Tim. 3:3, 8, Titus 1:7 and 2:3).
- **Carousing (or revelry).** Revelry has long been associated with idolatry, and especially the orgiastic or unrestrained worship of the gods of wine (such as Bacchus) and fertility (such as Artemis). Such practices often include music, dancing, drugs, alcohol, and uninhibited sensuality—similar to the modern "party," "kegger," or "rave." While today's carousing may not be directly associated with pagan religion, it is of the same spirit, and (as in ancient times) is a form of entertainment and hedonistic escapism (Rom. 13:13, 1 Peter 4:3).
- **And things like these.** It is not uncommon for someone today to argue, "But *my* [bad behavior] isn't on that list, so I should not be required to give it up." Such poor reasoning fails to recognize that Paul provides examples here, not an exhaustive, encyclopedic listing of every moral defect imaginable. "And things like these" (compare with "every form of evil" in 1 Thess. 5:22) is a dragnet that encompasses *any* worldly attitude or behavior inconsistent with the Spirit's teaching and influence.

Paul has warned the Galatians—and now warns again—"that those who practice such things will not inherit the kingdom of God" (5:21; see 1 Cor. 6:9–10). The Holy Spirit allows no mixture of godliness and wickedness; there is to be no sharing, communion, or fellowship between Christians and the satanic attitudes and practices of the world (2 Cor. 6:14—7:1). While the believer's *hope* in the kingdom is real and God guarantees it, actual entrance into the kingdom will not happen until he has remained faithful to the end (see 1 Cor. 15:50, 1 Thess. 2:12, 2 Tim. 4:18, 2 Peter 1:11, and Rev. 2:10). Not only must the believer identify and avoid these "deeds of the flesh," but he must put them to death—i.e., give them up entirely due to his allegiance to Christ. One cannot be led by the Holy Spirit who refuses to relinquish his worldly character (Rom. 8:12–14).

The Fruit of the Spirit (5:22–23): An unbeliever may practice "deeds of the flesh" naturally, even instinctively. One does not have to learn to restrain himself to practice them since they represent a *lack* of moral or dignified restraint. The "fruit of the Spirit," however, takes a considerable amount of time, deliberate effort, and self-control to produce. "Fruit" always takes time to mature and thus to reveal the true nature of the "tree" from which it came (Mat. 7:16–18, 12:33). The "deeds of the flesh" manifest themselves almost immediately; development of "fruit of the Spirit" requires a longer process. The reason for this slow development is because new converts have already been immersed in worldliness and need to be re-trained; this re-conditioning process involves a change in attitude as well as behavior; and even though they are "in Christ," converts are still influenced by old habits, old friends, and all-too-familiar temptations of their former lives. Recognizing this time factor should never serve as a license for failing to make strenuous effort to change, procrastination, or other baseless excuses.

"[F]ruit of the Spirit" means just that: the visible *produce* of the *Spirit's* influence upon the heart of the believer (5:22–23). It is not something we generate *for* God; it is that which He inspires and generates within us. All fruit (and growth, maturity, activity, light, and life) must be supplied by an external energy source. In this case, the Holy Spirit is the source of spiritual energy (or dynamic) that allows the believer to overcome his worldliness *and* internalize a completely different mindset and lifestyle instead.[93] Having put on the "new self" which is provided by God, he gradually but consistently changes from what he *was* into what God needs him to *be* (see Col. 3:1–10). Characteristics of this "new self" include:

- **Love.** Godly love [Greek, *agape*] is selfless, sacrificial, and always active. It is the hallmark of God's people and the binding force of the entire brotherhood (John 13:35, 1 Cor. 16:14, Col. 3:14, etc.). "God is love" (1 John 4:8), and those who are filled with His Spirit are filled with His love.
- **Joy.** God is not unhappy—He is filled with joy! It is true that He expresses wrath toward sin and those who choose to remain sinners,

---

93 For a much fuller discussion on this idea, I recommend my book, *The Holy Spirit of God: A Biblical Perspective* (Waynesville, OH: Spiritbuilding Publishers, 2010); go to www.spiritbuilding.com/chad.

but His wrath is not what *defines* Him. Instead, He is a God of warmth and delight. Those who obey His will in this life will enter the "joy of [their] Master" (Mat. 25:21). Such people are filled with His Spirit and experience joy even amid trials; it is for the joy of being with God that inspires them to obey Him (James 1:2–4, Heb. 12:1–3).

- **Peace.** This refers to the soul's calm repose because of its assurance of God's favor and His salvation (1 John 2:28), and not necessarily an absence of earthly conflict. Those who are united with God in faith are also at peace with Him, since unity and peace always exist (or fail to exist) together (Rom. 5:1–2, James 3:18).
- **Patience.** The Greek word here [*makrothymia*] is variously translated as longsuffering, forbearance, endurance, constancy, perseverance, and slowness in avenging wrongs.[94] The idea expressed is always that of staving off judgment (or, censure or punishment) in the anticipation of the offender's repentance and reform. Thus, God waits for (or shows patience toward) the sinner in hopes of his change of heart (Rom. 2:4, 2 Peter 3:9). Just as God shows us such patience, those who are led by the Spirit will show patience toward others (Col. 3:12–13).
- **Kindness.** This is a general term denoting all sorts of expressions of goodness, gentleness, or integrity. God's essential nature is exhibited in His kindness toward all men, both saints and sinners alike (Mat. 5:44–45). Those who are led by His Spirit also extend kindness and gentleness in dealing with others, and especially those in need of instruction (Eph. 4:2, 2 Tim. 2:25, James 3:13, and 1 Peter 3:15).
- **Goodness.** "Goodness" is another term with broad application; it is any virtue, beneficence, or uprightness of heart or conduct (i.e., righteousness). We know that God alone is truly "good" (Mat. 19:17) but those led by God will seek to imitate His goodness in their own behavior. His Spirit will bring about good in those who genuinely love the Lord (Rom. 8:28).
- **Faithfulness.** Faith, by itself, refers to one's personal convictions—the assurance of what he believes to be true. While God does not *make* a person faithful, He most certainly provides the *evidence* (or basis) for one's faith (Heb. 11:1–2) and can also ensure the *confidence* of it (Heb. 10:19–22). This knowledge or calm assurance of one's fellowship with

---

94 James Strong, *Strong's Talking Greek-Hebrew Dictionary*, electronic edition (database © WORDsearch Corp.), G3115.

God is a provision of His Spirit; a person cannot have such genuine assurance apart from being filled with Him.

- **Gentleness.** While similar to "kindness," this word does not refer so much to how a person conducts himself with others but expresses his overall demeanor or disposition (Mat. 11:29). Thus, this refers to one's mildness, humility, meekness, and quietness of spirit.
- **Self-control.** While it appears that self-control is something entirely dependent upon one's own effort (and not the Spirit's), the reason *for* and the strength to *practice* self-control is derived from the Spirit. Paradoxically, the believer *gains* control by *relinquishing* his own control to the Spirit's oversight. "Self-control" refers to discipline of character, temperance, and the structured and stable lifestyle of the believer; it is his mastery over his thoughts, conduct, emotions, and desires (2 Peter 1:6). The Spirit always leads a person in this direction and conditions the heart to accommodate this pursuit.

"[A]gainst such things there is no law" (5:23)—i.e., there is no boundary, restriction, or man-made legislation against such actions. The "fruit of the Spirit" cannot be constrained or defined by legal ordinances, human limitations, or earthly circumstances. No one can limit how much love, joy, peace, patience, etc. a person can have who is filled with God's Spirit.

Living by the Spirit (5:24–25): No one can produce "fruit of the Spirit" while in his unconverted, spiritually dead, and alienated state of being. He must die to what he *was* to become what God will *make* him. Thus, those who belong to Christ "have crucified the flesh" (5:24)—i.e., they have put to death the body of sin; they have died with Christ through the act of a water burial (baptism) (see Rom. 6:3–7, Gal. 2:20, and Col. 2:11–12). Formerly, the believer followed his human "passions and desires"; now he follows the Holy Spirit. The one whose soul is regenerated by the Holy Spirit (Titus 3:5) must also "walk" or visibly conduct himself in a manner consistent with this conversion (5:25). "The act by which Christ destroyed the old nature took place once, but the life of the believer must harmonize with what Christ has accomplished."[95] This new life must make no provision for boasting, rivalry, or ill-will (5:26; see Rom. 13:14); the new life is incompatible with the satanic deeds of the flesh.

---

95 JFB, *Commentary* (electronic), on 5:24.

Expectations for Those Led by the Spirit
(Gal. 6:1–10)

Dealing with Others' Struggles (6:1–5): "Brethren" (6:1) indicates a softening of Paul's tone toward the Galatians; he appeals to them on an equal plane. In this section, "you who are spiritual" refers to those who have not succumbed to the "bewitching" of the Judaizers (recall 3:1) but are walking by the Spirit. "Trespass" may refer to the sin of legalism or the practice of the deeds of the flesh; the expression here can include *any* trespass (or fault).

The goal of *all* discipline within the church must be that of *restoration*, not excommunication, and never vengeance. Even in the case of restoring an errant brother, the mature Christian will exercise a "spirit of gentleness [or, meekness]" since this is a fruit of the Spirit (recall 5:23). Meekness is not weakness or timidity but the willingness to patiently suffer injury or loss without seeking retaliation. "[E]ach one looking to yourself"—i.e., guarding against the temptation to sin (yourself) while dealing with someone else's sin. This may refer to the temptation to seek vengeance; boast in the fact that he (the restorer) has not sinned in the manner of his erring brother; become ensnared by the same sin as his fallen brother; etc. Dealing with sin requires mature experience, humble spirit, and proper self-examination. It is not a role for novices.

Instead of burdening themselves with the "yoke" of other men's impositions, Christians are to help bear the burdens of their struggling brothers and sisters in the Lord (6:2). Instead of taking upon themselves the Law of Moses, they are to fulfill (or complete) the "law of Christ." While the Law of Moses had 613 specific laws to observe (yes, the Jews counted them), the law of Christ has essentially two: love God with all your heart, soul, and mind; and love your "neighbor" (and specifically, your brother in Christ) as yourself (Mat. 22:37–40, Rom. 13:8–10). In other words, to fulfill the law of Christ is far easier (and more profitable) than trying to fulfill the Law of Moses. Just as Christ has borne all *our* burdens (Rom. 15:1–3), Christians are to help bear the burdens of their brethren.

Arrogance or self-righteous indignation toward those who have sinned is itself a sin; Paul sternly warns against this (6:3; see 1 Cor. 8:2–3). To think oneself as "something"—i.e., as one who is morally superior to his sinning brother, and that brother being beneath him—only manifests self-deception, not wisdom, compassion, or righteousness. He is, in fact, "nothing" of what he claims to be. If a Christian focuses on his own work (rather than comparing himself to the one caught in a trespass, for example), he will not boast "in regard to another" (6:4). Paul's comment, "then he will have reason for boasting in regard to himself alone," is intended as an exaggerated statement, not a doctrinal instruction. Elsewhere, Paul makes it clear that no believer should boast, except in Christ (Rom. 3:27, 1 Cor. 1:31, and Gal. 6:14).[96] In a sense, he is saying, "If you could make yourself perfect, then you would have something to boast about—but this will never happen."

"For each one will bear his own load" (6:5)—on the surface, this appears contradictory to what he just said in 6:2 (about bearing one another's burdens). Yet the focus here is on personal self-examination (and the recognition of one's moral responsibilities) rather than what he has to offer his brother in Christ. In other words, we help each other when and while we can, but none of us is exempt from moral responsibility and each of us will be held personally accountable for our actions (2 Cor. 5:10). This is as true for the erring brother as it is for the one who attempts to restore him.

Sowing and Reaping (6:6–10): To "share" (in 6:6) implies fellowship, communication, partnership, and a sharing of material possessions (as in Phil. 4:15). It is likely that Paul meant any or all these ideas: the recipient of the good news of salvation ought to reciprocate by blessing the one who brought him that message. In other words, no one is to take the (sharing of) the message for granted but ought to support the teachers of that message. Too often, those who are recipients of another person's experience, prolonged study, and trained abilities do not respond with proper gratitude or appreciation. Taking for granted what is given us is the path of least resistance; making effort to demonstrate sincere gratitude takes far more effort.

---

96 "Paul does not say, 'For if anyone imagines that he amounts to something he is deluding himself.' He says, 'For if anyone imagines that he amounts to something, *while he amounts to nothing*, he is deluding himself.' Paul is attacking the spirit of overconfidence in oneself" (Hendriksen, *NTC*, 233).

"Do not be deceived" (6:7)—there are numerous warnings against deception in the NT:

- Those who cause dissensions and hindrances within the church are those who "deceive the hearts of the unsuspecting" (Rom. 16:17–18).
- Those with inflated egos and who rest upon their own knowledge deceive themselves (1 Cor. 3:18).
- We are not to be deceived into thinking that the unrighteous will inherit the kingdom of God (1 Cor. 6:9).
- "Bad company corrupts good morals" (1 Cor. 15:33), and we are not to be deceived into thinking that any of us are invulnerable or immune to this.
- Those who allow themselves to be deceived with "empty words" incur the wrath of God (Eph. 5:6).
- "Let no one in any way deceive you" into thinking that Christ will come before the appointed time (2 Thess. 2:1–3).
- Evil men and impostors are those who both deceive and are deceived (2 Tim. 3:13).
- Enemies of the church are rebels, empty talkers, and deceivers (Titus 1:10).
- We are not to be deceived into thinking that God tempts people to sin, but each person is tempted by the lust of his own heart (James 1:13–16).
- One who claims to be religious but does not bridle his own tongue deceives himself (James 1:26).
- John's first epistle was written in response to those who were trying to deceive Christians (1 John 2:26).
- It is a deception to think that one who does not *practice* righteousness will *be* righteous (1 John 3:7).
- Those who deny the divinity of Jesus are deceivers and "antichrists" (2 John 1:7).
- Satan (the "great dragon") is the one who "deceives the whole world" (Rev. 12:9).
- Those who succumb to Satan's deceptions will join in his ultimate demise (Rev. 19:20, 20:10).

These strong and persistent warnings, while pertaining to unbelievers, are *given* to believers. Part of teaching the salvation and blessings of the gospel includes teaching its warnings and admonitions. "God is not mocked" does not mean people will not mock Him at all, for they certainly do. However, their mocking does not injure Him but will most certainly lead to their own ruin. To "mock" God means to (attempt to) pervert His system of justice by seeking to gain an advantage from evil conduct. In the natural world, this does not work: whatever plant's seed is sown brings that same plant out of the ground. In the spiritual realm, the principle is the same: whatever "seed" a person sows in his heart brings forth a spiritual character consistent with that seed. Engaging in "deeds of the flesh" will never bring about "fruit of the Spirit"; likewise, the Galatians cannot live by self-justification and expect to be saved by grace (6:8). No one mocks God with impunity. In the end, God will destroy the mockers, unbelievers, and disobedient (2 Thess. 1:6–10).

Sowing seed is one thing; having the patient endurance to wait for the result (or harvest) of what is sown is quite another (Heb. 10:35–39, James 5:7–11). As in any other difficult endeavor, many people begin the journey with good expectations but do not persevere until the end (6:9–10). Therefore, Paul encourages the Galatians (and all believers) not to "lose heart" (or "grow weary") of doing good: the harvest will come in due time, and those who have sown to the Spirit will reap that which the Spirit has safeguarded for them (Eph. 1:13–14, Heb. 13:16). Succumbing to discouragement or despair will forfeit their grand reward. Life is short, however, and no one knows his own future; the right thing to do, then, is to "do good" at every opportunity. The recipients of our good deeds are "all people"—i.e., regardless of whether one is a Christian. On the other hand, believers have a *special* obligation to help members of the spiritual family of God. If a believer is unwilling (or simply neglects) to help his own brother or sister in Christ, his religion is worthless (James 1:22–27, 1 John 3:17–18).

Concluding Remarks
(Gal. 6:11–18)

This has been a difficult epistle for Paul to write. He has had to say strong words to those who are misrepresenting the gospel, yet he has balanced this with compassion and concern for the Galatians themselves. Likely, Paul dictated this epistle to one of his fellow workers until this point; the conclusion, however, he writes in his own hand—and with a definite change in the size of the lettering (6:11; see Rom. 16:22 and 1 Cor. 16:21). This is Paul's way of personalizing the letter and is also his stamp of authenticity. Some scholars have assumed that the "large letters" are due to Paul's allegedly poor eyesight (see comments on 4:13–15), but this remains conjecture. Likely, it is to draw special emphasis to his closing remarks.

The Judaizers' True Intentions (6:12–13): To summarize what he has already said (in so many words), Paul explains the true intentions of the Judaizers: they are not genuinely seeking to obey the gospel but want to make the Gentile converts into Jewish proselytes (6:12). This would prevent them from being persecuted from the hard-line Jewish purists while allegedly maintaining a good standing among the Christian churches—in essence, straddling the fence. In doing so, they compromise salvation by faith for a "good showing in the flesh"—i.e., circumcision and other visible acts of self-justification. While even the non-Christian Jewish purists did not keep the Law of Moses perfectly, they wanted to impose upon others to exercise control over them (6:13; see Acts 15:7–10). To "boast in your flesh" means to take credit for making Gentile converts their followers. "There [on the cross] man did his worst against God while God did His best in behalf of man... They [Judaizers] denied the cross so that they would not have to bear a cross...."[97]

Paul's Genuine Servitude (6:14–18): In sharp contrast, Paul's boast was in the work of Christ, not human effort (6:14). No amount of religious legalism, law-keeping, or human effort can redeem human souls. The "cross of Christ" is the only genuine reason for one's boast; the redemptive work of Christ is to be the pride of every Christian. "The world has been crucified to me, and I to the world" is the same thought that Paul expressed earlier (2:20,

---

97 Strauss, *Devotional Studies*, 100; bracketed words are mine.

5:24), but in slightly different words. Again, Paul refers to the complete (spiritual) separation from the world and its corruption, as symbolized through his own death-burial-resurrection demonstration of water baptism (see 1 Peter 3:21–22 and 2 Peter 1:4). In effect, the world no longer is Paul's master, and he is no longer a slave to the world (Rom. 6:11).

Paul makes a profound, once-and-for-all declaration about circumcision (and all such legal impositions): it makes no difference whether one receives this (6:15). One is not made *more* righteous if he is circumcised; he is no *less* a child of God if he is not. What matters to God—and thus what should matter to Christians—is one's "new creation" in Christ (see 2 Cor. 5:17, Eph. 2:10, Col. 2:9–12, etc.) and his faithful obedience to Him. "Circumcision is nothing, and uncircumcision is nothing, but what matters is the keeping of the commandments of God" (1 Cor. 7:19). No one is saved by what he does for himself; he is only saved because of his faith in what *Christ* does for him. Those who "walk according to this rule [lit., line up with this principle]" will receive divine mercy and enjoy the peace of a right relationship with God (6:16). "Israel of God" refers no longer to those who are physical descendants of Jacob (a.k.a. Israel) but those who are spiritual descendants of Abraham—i.e., Christ's church (recall 3:29; see Rom. 9:6–8). While the Judaizers wanted to bind Gentile believers to their own heritage, physical lineages are rendered "obsolete" in Christ (Heb. 8:13). Indeed, God's judgment upon Jerusalem (in AD 70) would underscore this point once and for all.

"From now on let no one cause trouble for me" (6:17)—i.e., let none of you (Galatians) question my apostolic authority. Such failure to submit to this authority served as a source of grief for Paul (cf. Heb. 13:17). As a bearer of the "brand-marks of Jesus," Paul has demonstrated his willingness to suffer for the gospel among unbelievers; he should not have to endure suffering from his own Christian brethren. In ancient times, slaves were marked with branding irons to indicate the master to whom they belonged; likewise, Paul bore the marks of his identity with his Master.[98] This idea is intentionally set against the mark (or physical showing) of circumcision. It is better, he

---

98 The great extent of Paul's sufferings certainly left their literal marks upon his physical body (2 Cor. 11:23–27).

implies, to bear the brand-marks of servitude to Christ than to receive the proud mark of Judaism.

After having said these strong words, Paul ends by appealing to the Galatian Christians as "brethren" (6:18). He wishes upon them the "grace of our Lord Jesus Christ"—grace that cannot be earned, merited, or obtained through any human accomplishment but is imparted only through one's faith in the Lord.

Sources Used for *Quick Study Commentary: Galatians*

Barnes, Albert. *Barnes' Notes*, vol. 11. Grand Rapids: Baker Books, 1987.

Coffman, James Burton. *Commentary on Galatians, Ephesians, Philippians, Colossians.* Austin, TX: Firm Foundation, 1977.

Conybeare, W. J. and J. S. Howson. *The Life and Epistles of St. Paul.* Grand Rapids: Eerdmans, 1964.

Findlay, George G. "Galatians, Epistle to." *The International Standard Bible Encyclopedia*, vol. 2, James Orr, ed. Grand Rapids: Eerdmans Publishing Co., 1939.

Hendriksen, William. *New Testament Commentary: Galatians, Ephesians, Philippians, Colossians and Philemon.* Grand Rapids: Baker Books, 1995.

Huxtable, E. "Galatians"; includes "Introduction," Dissertations. *The Pulpit Commentary* (vol. 20), H. D. Spence and Joseph S. Exell, eds. Peabody, MS: Hendrickson Publishing [no date; orig., 1897].

Jamieson, Robert, Andrew Fausset and David Brown. *Commentary Critical and Explanatory on the Whole Bible (1871)*, electronic edition. Database © 2012 by WORDsearch Corp.

Lenski, R. C. H. *Commentary on the New Testament: The Interpretation of St. Paul's Epistles to the Galatians, to the Ephesians, and to the Philippians* (vol. 8). Peabody, MA: Hendrickson Publishers, 1998 [orig., Lutheran Book Concern, 1937].

Lipscomb, David. *A Commentary on the New Testament Epistles, volume III: Second Corinthians and Galatians* (J. W. Shepherd, ed.). Nashville: Gospel Advocate Co., 1979.

Peterson, L. M. "Galatians, Epistle to." *The Zondervan Pictorial Encyclopedia of the Bible* (vol. 2), Merrill C. Tenney, ed. Grand Rapids: Zondervan, 1976.

Ramsay, William. *The Cities of St. Paul.* Whitefish, MT: Kessinger Publishing, 2004.

Robertson, Archibald T. *Word Pictures in the New Testament*, vol. 4. Grand Rapids: Baker Books, 1931.

Strauss, Lehman. *Devotional Studies in Galatians and Ephesians.* Neptune, NJ: Loizeaux Bros., 1957.

Strong, James. *Strong's Talking Greek-Hebrew Dictionary*, electronic edition. Database © WORDsearch Corp.

Sychtysz, Chad. *The Holy Spirit of God: A Biblical Perspective.* Waynesville, OH: Spiritbuilding Publishers, 2010.

Tenney, Merrill C. *Galatians: The Charter of Christian Liberty.* Grand Rapids: Wm. B. Eerdmans Publishing Co., 1957 (paperback edition, 1989).

Thayer, Joseph. ***Thayer's Greek Definitions***, electronic edition. © 2009 QuickVerse.

Wharton, Edward C. *Freed for Freedom: Studies in Galatians.* Nashville, TN: 21st Century Christian, 1995.

Scripture taken from the NEW AMERICAN STANDARD BIBLE ®, Copyright © 1960, 1962, 1963, 1968, 1971, 1972, 1973, 1975, 1977, 1995 by The Lockman Foundation. Used by permission.

⇒ **End of *Quick Study Commentary: Galatians*** ⇐

Introduction to *Ephesians*

The *Epistle to the Ephesians* "is one of the most magnificent" letters of the New Testament (NT), "containing the very essence of Christianity."[99] We cannot overestimate its value to our understanding of Christian doctrine—and especially that of Christ's church. "[It] has been called 'the divinest composition of man,' 'the distilled essence of the Christian religion,' 'the most authoritative and most consummate compendium of the Christians faith,' 'full to the brim with thoughts and doctrines sublime and momentous,' etc."[100]

Ephesians was written by the apostle Paul—this has rarely been disputed—around AD 60–61, while Paul was in Roman custody following his arrest in Jerusalem. It is unclear whether he was still in Caesarea at the time of this writing, or if he had already been transported to Rome. Regardless, he is clearly in prison (3:1, 4:1, and 6:20), and thus *Ephesians* has long been identified as one of the "prison epistles" along with *Philippians*, *Colossians*, and *Philemon*. The epistle opens with, "To the saints who are at Ephesus" (1:1)—yet "at Ephesus" is not in some of the oldest manuscripts. Some believe that this epistle was written to Laodicea, based upon Col. 4:16, yet this lacks any direct proof.[101] Others believe it was an encyclical letter designed to be read by a number of churches, and thus explains the absence of any specific names, salutations, or historical references.[102] Hendriksen believes it to have been written for Ephesus originally, but intended to be circulated after that.[103] Lenski is adamant that this epistle was written specifically to Ephesus; "The entire early church regarded this as a letter than had been sent to the Ephesians by Paul."[104]

---

[99] James Coffman, *Commentary on Galatians, Ephesians, Philippians, Colossians* (Austin, TX: Firm Foundation, 1977), 122.

[100] William Hendriksen, *New Testament Commentary: Galatians, Ephesians, Philippians, Colossians and Philemon* (Grand Rapids: Baker Books, 1995), 32.

[101] W. J. Conybeare and J. S. Howson, *The Life and Epistles of St. Paul* (Grand Rapids: Eerdmans, 1964), 702–703; bracketed word is mine.

[102] Robert Jamieson, Andrew Fausset and David Brown. *Commentary Critical and Explanatory on the Whole Bible (1871)* (database © 2012 by WORDsearch Corp.), on 1:1.

[103] Hendriksen, *NTC*, 61.

[104] R. C. H. Lenski, *Commentary on the New Testament: The Interpretation of St. Paul's Epistles to the Galatians, to the Ephesians, and to the Philippians*, vol. 8 (Peabody, MA:

In Paul's day, Ephesus was the capital city of Asia Minor, built in antiquity in the valley of the Cayster River. For centuries, the predominance of other cities overshadowed it, but the city rose to its zenith during the Roman period. It boasted one of the best harbors of the province and was one of the easiest cities to access by land and sea. Its prime location made it an excellent hub for dispersing the gospel throughout the entire Roman Empire.

> In the time of St. Paul it [Ephesus] was the greatest city of Asia Minor, as well as the metropolis of the *province* of Asia. Though Greek in its origin, it was half-oriental in the prevalent worship, and in the character of its inhabitants; and being constantly visited by ships from all parts of the Mediterranean, and united by great roads with the markets of the interior, it was the common meeting-place of various characters and classes of men.[105]

Paul had spent considerable time (up to three years) in Ephesus during his third missionary journey (Acts 19, 20:31). Having little success in its Jewish synagogues, he taught in a school of Tyrannus for some time which allowed him to wield considerable influence over the Gentiles within the city (Acts 19:8–10). It was also in Ephesus that Paul performed "extraordinary miracles" to demonstrate the real and irrefutable power of God among a pagan and superstitious people (Acts 19:11–12).

Ephesus was the seat of the worship of Diana [Greek: Artemis]—a kind of Greek-Oriental goddess of fertility for which the people had constructed one of the greatest temples to have ever been built. This Temple of Diana was enormous and magnificent: 425' long and 220' wide, its roof was held up by 127 columns of marble rising 60' high. It took 220 years to build this structure. "It is probable that there was no religious building in the world in which was concentrated a greater amount of admiration, enthusiasm, and superstition."[106]

Hendrickson Publishers, 1998), 332. He also dismisses the idea that the lack of a personal salutation implies anything, and notes that *2 Corinthians, Galatians*, and *1 & 2 Thessalonians* also lack such salutations. "To regard our epistle as an encyclical because it lacks greetings is thus unwarranted" (334).

105 Conybeare and Howson, *Life and Epistles*, 369; emphasis is theirs.

106 Ibid., 423.

Ephesus was also renowned for its practice of magic and sorcery. So-called "Ephesian letters" were engraved on the statue of Diana; pronouncing these letters would allegedly act as a charm that harnessed the power of evil spirits; when written, they worked as an amulet or talisman.[107] The burning of the books of magic arts during Paul's stay in that city gives but a small sampling of the full number of books and written spells that must have existed at that time (Acts 19:19). Thus, against the backdrop of pagan worship and sorcery, Paul wrote about the *true* temple—an otherworldly, indestructible, and far more beautiful temple (Christ's church) than that of Diana—and *true* works of divine power—the resurrection of "dead" souls to walk in fellowship with the Sovereign God of heaven. These contrasts, while not expressed in the epistle, seem quite intentional.

Purpose and Theme: *Ephesians* is divided into two equal parts, the first part addressing the doctrine (or theology) of Christ and His church, the second addressing the practical application of this doctrine. It has been said that the theme of *Ephesians* is "the church of Christ," while that of *Colossians* (its sister epistle) is "the Christ of the church."[108] However, the letter is not solely about the church but is more about the *need for human redemption* which is fulfilled *through God's wisdom* (His revealed purpose). When people conform to God's eternal purpose (3:11), He brings them into the body of those who have also conformed, which is the source of all spiritual blessings—the church that Jesus built.[109]

Paul's purpose for writing *Ephesians* is manifold. The overarching purpose is the apostle's desire to expound upon God's plan of redemption and how it so perfectly fulfills man's spiritual needs. Purposes related to this are evident in Paul's two prayers that he offers in the epistle (1:15–21, 3:14–19). In essence, he prayed that the Ephesian Christians' hearts would be open to God's will; they would be filled with spiritual knowledge; they would live in anticipation of God's spiritual inheritance and trust in His ability to fulfill this promise; they would be renewed by the power of God's Spirit; and they "may be filled up to all the fullness of God." Themes related to these prayers are as follows:

---

107 Ibid., 371.

108 Paraphrased from A T. Robertson, *Word Pictures in the New Testament*, vol. 4 (Grand Rapids: Baker Books, 1931), 515.

109 Harry Pickup, Jr., class notes (August 2–5, 2004).

- The spiritual **church of Christ** (1:3—3:12)—its predestination, purpose, heavenly glory, and providential protection. Paul identifies the church as God's temple, God's household, a dwelling of God, Christ's body, Christ's bride, the "one new man," and simply "the church"—and *all* these expressions are summed up in the phrase "in Christ." *Ephesians* provides some of the finest exposition on Christ's church that exists in the NT.
- **"in Christ"** (or "in Him") occurs some 30 times in this epistle, illustrating the spiritual context or state of being of those who have been redeemed. Such people are not defined by race, geography, or earthly status, but by their spiritual identity with Christ Himself, having been redeemed by His blood (1:7).
- The saving **grace of God**—a recurring subject in this epistle—is imparted only to those who are in Christ's church. His church, then, is the work of God rather than the result of human effort (2:8–10); the spiritual nature of this body transcends all human or earthly limitations (2:19–22).
- A **regenerated life**—the "new self"—is the result of having been added to Christ's church. This new life is characterized by the removal of old sinful thinking and habits, as well as the presence of Christ-like thinking and godly habits (4:17—5:21).
- All earthly relationships in which Christians participate must be recalibrated to accommodate the **"new self"** and its wholesome attitude. In marriage, home, and society, Christians are instructed to walk "in a manner worthy of the calling with which you have been called" (4:1). This "walk" must be conducted "as to the Lord," "because we are members of His body," and as "slaves of Christ" (5:22, 30, and 6:6).
- Paul concludes the letter with a militaristic portrayal of the **Christian's battle** against the "spiritual forces of wickedness in the heavenly places" (6:10–17). This battle really belongs to the Lord, and thus each member of Christ's body is to put on the "full armor of God" in preparation for it. The entire church of Christ is seen as one great warrior fighting against one great enemy (Satan) yet armored in such as way as to prevent it from succumbing to his assaults.

Much more on the themes of *Ephesians* will be addressed in the following exposition.

General Outline of *Ephesians*

- **Section One: Praise to God for His Church (1:1–23)**
    - Salutation (1:1–2)
    - Hymn of Praise to God (1:3–14)
    - Paul's First Prayer for the Ephesians (1:15–23)
- **Section Two: Universal Salvation in Christ (2:1—3:21)**
    - Salvation by Grace through Faith (2:1–10)
    - The "One New Man" in Christ (2:11–22)
    - Paul's Ministry to the Revealed Gospel (3:1–13)
    - Paul's Second Prayer for the Ephesians (3:14–21)
- **Section Three: The Unity of Christ's Body (4:1–16)**
    - The Unity of the Spirit (4:1–6)
    - Christ's Gifts to His Church (4:7–16)
- **Section Four: The Christian's Walk (4:17—6:9)**
    - Putting on the "New Self" (4:17–24)
    - Not That, But This (4:25—5:21)
    - The Marriage Relationship (5:22–33)
    - Other Relationships (6:1–9)
- **Section Five: The Christian's Struggle with the Unseen World (6:10–20)**
- **Concluding Remarks (6:21–24)**

SECTION ONE:
PRAISE TO GOD FOR HIS CHURCH
(1:1–23)

Salutation
(Eph. 1:1–2)

With a standard introduction found in most of his epistles, Paul affirms his apostleship and the source of authority with which he speaks (1:1). It was not Paul's decision to become an apostle; Christ commissioned him (1 Cor. 1:1) and God had set him apart for this very purpose (Gal. 1:1, 15). This epistle is written "to the saints"—lit., holy ones [Greek, *hagios*], and so for the more than sixty times the word "saints" is used in the NT. The words "at Ephesus" are not in three of the earliest manuscripts of the NT, leading scholars to believe that this may have been a general epistle intended to be distributed throughout the churches.[110] The "faithful in Christ Jesus" is not a separate group of people than "saints" but simply another designation for them. "Grace to you and peace"—Paul's standard yet sincere form of greeting for the churches. Grace *from* God and peace *with* God are mutually dependent blessings: for one to exist, the other must be present. Paul cannot confer divine grace upon anyone—this is God's business—but he can speak his earnest desire for the Ephesians, namely, that they be immersed in His grace and thus will be at peace with Him (Rom. 5:1–2).

A Hymn of Praise to God
(Eph. 1:3–14)

In the Greek text, 1:3–14 is one unbroken sentence. The predominant thought in this section concerns the *planning, work,* and *cooperation* of the triune Godhead in producing a divinely protected body of believers that will receive eternal glory. Thus, the Father has predestined this body (1:3–5); it is summed up (or brought to its fulfillment) in Jesus Christ (1:9–10); and it is "sealed with the Holy Spirit of promise" (1:13). The church of Christ—the

---

110 JFB, *Commentary* (electronic), on 1:1; Roy Cogdill, *The New Testament: Book by Book* (Marion, IN: Cogdill Foundation Publications, 1975), 74; see "Introduction" of this study.

spiritual body of believers brought together "in Christ" by grace and through faith—was not planned by men, was not a work of men, and its success does not rest upon the cooperation of men. The hope of those who are redeemed is supported by nothing less than the authority and power of God Himself—God the Father, God the Son, and God the Spirit.

The Predestination of Christ's Church (1:3–6): "Blessed be the God and Father" (1:3)—praise to God is fitting and expected from those who are righteous (Psalm 33:1). The Father is the Source of all love, blessings, and salvation; He deserves praise for this (Rev. 4:9–11). However, the context in which the Father confers spiritual blessings upon people is through Christ: one who is "in Christ" is a recipient of God's fellowship; otherwise, he remains outside of God's fellowship (to be discussed in chapter 2). "[E]very spiritual blessing" speaks of the saving grace of God in all its forms: everything God bestows upon the human soul to bring it to glory. "[I]n the heavenly {places}" refers to the spiritual nature (or context) of such blessings, as opposed to the general kindness (or beneficence) that God bestows upon all people, regardless of their standing with Him (as in Mat. 5:45).[111] These spiritual blessings (and salvation itself) are only "in Christ": they are nowhere else; and no other means will obtain them (John 14:6). Those who seek to find fellowship with God through the agency of men, man-made religion, mystical knowledge, personal merit, or any other means are being deceived into believing that *human effort* can equal or replace *divine grace.*

The body of believers (the recipients of "every spiritual blessing") is not a self-chosen group of human souls but one which God had designated from the beginning to belong to Him (1:4–5; see Acts 20:28, 1 Cor. 6:19–20, and Titus 2:14). "Predestined" means "marked out (or chosen) beforehand" or "foreordained." Yet when Paul speaks of predestination here (as in Rom. 8:29–30) he refers to a *group* of people and not individual souls. The predestined group here is Christ's church: only His church has been predestined for glory "before the foundation of the world." No *other* group has been chosen or appointed by God to receive salvation and every spiritual blessing. Before God created the physical universe, He had already

---

111 "This remarkable expression occurs five times in this epistle (1:3, 20; 2:6; 3:10; 6:12) and nowhere else" (Coffman, *Commentary*, 128–129).

determined that the church would enjoy a holy union with His Son.[112] One becomes part *of* this church when God invites him through His word and His Spirit (2 Thess. 2:13–14) *and* that person responds rightly to this invitation through personal obedience.[113] Only those who are *made* "holy and blameless" *and* continue to live in conformity to this state of being will be included in this glorified body of believers (see Phil. 2:15, Col. 1:21–22, 1 Peter 1:13–16, 1 John 3:1–3, etc.).

The words "in love" should be connected to 1:5: the Father's love initiated and provided for our salvation, not our love for the Father (see 2:4–5, 1 John 4:10, 19). Thus, "in love, He predestined us to adoption as sons through Jesus Christ to Himself" (1:5): believers are made "sons" of God through adoption and not natural sonship. We are a part of God's physical Creation by means of a flesh-and-blood existence; but we must be "born of God" (or "born again") to identify with the predestined body of Christ (John 1:12–13, 3:5). Adoption is a legal process that serves several purposes:

- Believers are brought into God's household (i.e., made a part of His holy family). This allows us all the privileges of sonship and separates us from those who are not identified with God (Mat. 7:21, John 8:35, 2 Cor. 6:17–18, etc.).
- Believers are identified with God, given a distinctive name ("Christians" or "saints"), and thus distinguished from those who give highest allegiance to any other name (Acts 4:12, 2 Tim. 2:19, 1 Peter 4:16, Rev. 3:12, 14:1, etc.).

---

112 "God chose Christ and God chose the church. The church is composed of individuals who come into Christ by responding to the conditions of the gospel and who remain devoted to him. God did not choose the individuals unconditionally apart from their own voluntary choice to live as a part of Christ's body. God chose to save all in the class who truly comply with his will. He chose to save all who faithfully serve him in Christ" (C. G. Caldwell, *Truth Commentaries: Ephesians* [Bowling Green, KY: Guardian of Truth Foundation, 1994], 19.

113 Christ's church incorporates all those who had lived (and died) in faith prior to the establishment of His church. Jesus' salvation is not just for those who are called Christians, but for all whom God has justified since the beginning of mankind. Since all such justification comes through the same means—namely, the blood of Christ (Rom. 3:23–25)—we could literally say that everyone who has been saved is "in Christ."

- Believers are eligible for a legal inheritance provided by God and ensured by His Holy Spirit. This inheritance is really Christ's inheritance which He shares with us, as He has inherited all things.

To the Praise of God's Glory (1:7–11): Thus, everything God has done for His church is proper, legitimate, and honorable. It was through the "kind intention of His will" that the church enjoys such hope and privileges; in other words, God *desires* to provide salvation for humankind and *longs* to bring believers into fellowship with Him. All this God did for the church "to the praise of His glory" (1:6)—a phrase used three times in this section (1:12, 14). Everything God does—and especially as a demonstration of His divine grace—warrants praise and adoration from those who love God and worship Him in spirit and truth (John 4:23–24). His glory, majesty, and sovereign decisions ought to elicit humble praise from the recipients of His grace. The reason why we can benefit from His glory is because of "the Beloved"—the Son of God Himself (Mat. 12:18; in Col. 1:13, "the Son of His love").

The church of Christ is a blood-bought people (1:7). Earthly wealth or human effort cannot redeem sinful souls (1 Peter 1:18–19). "Redemption [Greek, *apolutrosin*] is deliverance or release from any form of bondage upon payment of a ransom."[114] Redemption comes by way of One (Christ) who intimately identifies with those whom He has redeemed *and yet* is superior to them. He secures our redemption through His blood, since it is "by reason of the life [within blood] that makes atonement" possible (Lev. 17:10–11, bracketed words added). According to the Law of Moses, an Israelite who was, because of his extreme poverty, hopelessly enslaved to another Israelite could be purchased out of that slavery by a close relative (Lev. 25:47–49). Jesus became flesh and blood to identify with those enslaved to sin (John 8:34, Heb. 2:10–15), thus fulfilling that "type" prophecy of the Law. With redemption comes forgiveness, and wherever is forgiveness must be saving grace.[115] Believers are not given a thimbleful of grace, but God's gifts—forgiveness and every spiritual blessing—are "lavished upon us" (1:8).

---

114 Caldwell, *Ephesians*, 26.

115 "The word Paul used here for 'forgiveness' is *aphesis*, used by him in only two other passages (Rom. 4:7; Col. 1:14). It means 'letting go,' not 'exacting payment for'" (William Taylor, quoted in Coffman, *Commentary*, 137).

In other words, Christ does not just give a small bit of hope but gives life abundantly (John 10:10).

Through God's wisdom and insight—for grace is God's plan and not ours—He "made known to us the mystery of His will" (1:8–9). Paul will explain this "mystery" in chapter 3; for now, his focus is on what God has accomplished through Jesus Christ. Such accomplishments were carried out (or summed up) with a specific purpose in mind, according to a specific plan (1:9–10). "Administration [or, stewardship; lit., household economy]" here refers to the overarching work of Christ as conducted *in* His church and *for* His church—a ministry "suitable to the fullness of the times" (Gal. 4:4). Christ did not build His church a minute too early or too late; its design is flawless and incorruptible; He used no inferior products in its construction. In other words, He established it at the right time in human history, for all the right reasons, and with all the right materials (so to speak). In all He accomplished as the world's redeemer, Christ did everything necessary "in the heavens and … on the earth"—that is, in the invisible as well as the visible worlds. "Sin has caused disorder in the relationship of all creation to God, but Christ has provided the means … by which that order may be restored."[116]

Because of His once-for-all performance, Christ was able to secure an inheritance for the one group that God has predestined *for* this glory: His church (1:11). All provisions for this inheritance were by "the counsel of His will"—i.e., according to the eternal desire of God's heart; this is what He has always wanted. This priceless reward is only for those "in Him," those redeemed by Christ's blood and forgiven by God's grace. Everything having to do with human salvation has been carefully planned, organized, and executed by God; nothing humanly impossible has been left to human effort.

Sealed by the Holy Spirit (1:12–14): The Jews were "the first to hope in Christ" (1:12) since they were the first to hear the gospel's proclamation. Since the gospel is the fulfillment of the many promises which faithful Israelites kept alive for centuries, it was only right that they should be the first to receive the realization of those promises (Luke 1:68–75, Acts 3:25, and Rom. 1:16). But "in Him, you also"—i.e., you Gentiles also—have the

---

116 JFB, *Commentary* (electronic), on 1:10.

same opportunity for salvation and are eligible for the same inheritance (1:13–14). Notice the order in which this eligibility is secured:

- They **listened** to "the message of truth, the gospel of your salvation." No one can be saved by a gospel which he has never heard; faith comes through *hearing* the gospel, and never apart from it. We do not have a single instance in the NT where a person was saved (or even could be saved) without first hearing the gospel *of* his salvation.
- Having heard, they also **believed** in that gospel. "Believe" here means "to be obedient to"; this is necessarily implied in the context, as in many other citations in Scripture (cf. John 3:16 and 3:36, for example). Sinners need to hear the gospel, but hearing is insufficient by itself. Unless a person acts *in faith* according to what he has heard, his "hearing" is useless. God will not approve of anyone who will not act in faith to what He has provided the hearer (Heb. 4:2, 11:1–2, 6).
- Having believed, they were then "sealed in Him" or **identified with Christ**. Everyone who calls upon the name of the Lord is thus *known* by Him in a new and special manner (1 Cor. 8:3); "The firm foundation of God stands, having this seal, 'The Lord knows those who are His'" (2 Tim. 2:19; see Rev. 7:1–3 for a symbolic portrayal of this sealing). The means or agency of this sealing is the giving of His Holy Spirit. This is not for the purpose of performing miracles—Paul is discussing *salvation in Christ*, not the ability to work miracles—but to provide believers with access to the Father (see 2:18) and whatever other spiritual help the Spirit provides (see 2 Cor. 1:21–22 and 5:5). "The Spirit is a living seal, thus a mark that is proper for the divine life kindled in us."[117]
- Having been sealed, believers are **given a living hope of future inheritance**—i.e., they will literally "see" their redemption rather than simply having *faith* that it exists. This "view to the redemption of God's

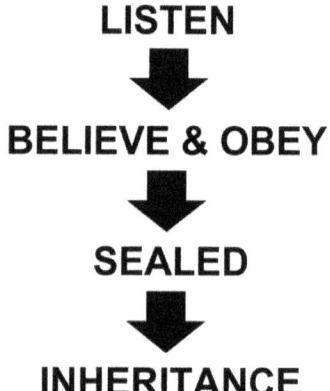

LISTEN
⬇
BELIEVE & OBEY
⬇
SEALED
⬇
INHERITANCE

---

117 Lenski, *Interpretation*, 384.

own possession" refers to the church's afterworld glory, having served the Lord faithfully while upon this earth (Rev. 19:7–8). "The Spirit is the first down payment of our inheritance and makes certain that in due time the inheritance in full will be turned over to us."[118]

All this—the summing up of all things in Christ, the salvation of Jews and Gentiles, and the future grandeur of the redeemed body of Christ—are "to the praise of His glory." All that God does, and all that people do in response to what He does, contributes to His sovereign majesty and splendor.

Paul's First Prayer for the Ephesians (Eph. 1:15–23)

Like the preceding doxology (1:3–14), so 1:15–23 is also one unbroken sentence in the Greek text. "[H]aving heard of the faith that exists among you" (1:15) may seem awkward if Paul was the one who *brought* the gospel to these people in the first place (Acts 19). But it does not say in *Acts* that Paul was the first to proclaim the gospel in Ephesus, only that he spent a considerable amount of time and effort *building the church* there. Regardless, the reputation of the Ephesian Christians had circulated throughout the brotherhood, so that Paul both *knew personally* and *had heard from others* of their faith and love.[119]

Paul's Prayer (1:16–21): To support their godly endeavor, Paul offers a personal prayer on their behalf—a prayer of *thanks* and a petition for *divine help* (1:16–17). This help would be in the form of "a spirit of wisdom and of revelation in the knowledge of Him"—i.e., wisdom that God alone can impart (see James 1:5) and a richer, more enlightened understanding of His will (see 5:15–17). While this might appear to refer specifically to *miraculous* gifts, nothing in the context supports this. The emphasis here is on what God provides (or imparts) rather than what believers can obtain or acquire alone. If Christians do not believe that God contributes to their spiritual growth

---

118 *Ibid.*, 385.

119 The same expression is used in Phile. 5 concerning the man (Philemon) whom Paul most certainly knew before he wrote those words.

apart from human effort, we have no reason to pray to Him or ask for His help on anything.

Having described his general petition to God on the Ephesians' behalf, Paul becomes much more specific in his request (1:18–19a). He asks that God would enlighten their hearts to the great hope that they have in Him; the priceless inheritance that awaits all the saints in Christ; and the immeasurable power which God employs on behalf of His people. God pours out this hope, riches, and power within His church—"toward us who believe." Such spiritual strength is the same which filled Christ during His ministry and raised Him from the grave (1:19b–20; see Rom. 8:11). "If we kept silent about the resurrection, we would not be speaking of God."[120] Because of what Christ has personally accomplished, the church can have great confidence in its own future. Our Savior has ascended into the presence of the Father and taken His seat at His right hand (Acts 2:33, Heb. 8:1–2, etc.)[121]; the church can rest assured that it, too, will one day be exalted in glory and dwell in "the heavenly {places}."[122]

Christ's rule over God's kingdom is unparalleled, unchallengeable, and incorruptible (1:21; see 1 Peter 3:21–22). He is not trying to gain supremacy over His enemies but is already far above them in power and authority.[123] "Authority" is a most underrated subject among Christians today; the failure

---

120 Quoted in Coffman, *Commentary*, 146.

121 "The right hand [Greek, *dexia*] is a symbolic phrase denoting authority, degree of position, or level of rank. It indicates the closeness of relationship between Christ and the Father. It speaks of the superiority of Christ to all other spiritual (and earthly) beings. It is not a material place or a literal location for God is not a material Being (John 4:24). That is further made obvious by the phrase 'heavenly places' meaning 'in the spiritual realm'" (Caldwell, *Ephesians*, 59).

122 Jesus promised His disciples that He would "prepare a place" for them and usher them to that "place" (John 14:1–3). He also entered the holy sanctuary of God upon His ascension into heaven (Heb. 9:11–12). The point is: whatever heaven is, it is not merely a state of conscious existence but a very real "place" (or destination) to which the believer longs to go. It is not a physical place in which flesh and blood can enter (1 Cor. 15:50, 53), but this does not mean it is not *real*. A spiritual dwelling is no less real than a physical one; in fact, it is even *more* real in the fact of its glory, endurance, and indestructibility (2 Cor. 4:18).

123 "Sitting expresses permanency. The expression 'the right hand' is God's infinite glory, power, and majesty, which the risen and exalted Christ exercises completely. In the state of humiliation he exercised these powers only to the degree that they were necessary for his redemptive work; now he exercises them in an infinite way" (Lenski, *Interpretation*, 400).

to appreciate and honor authority is the primary reason for the wide array of pseudo-Christian religions and other deviations from sound doctrine. Christ's authority is not simply a matter of formality or protocol; He is not a mere ornamental fixture upon the throne of God. Instead, His authority is a matter of *salvation* to the one who obeys Him, and *condemnation* to the one who disobeys (or fails to believe in) Him. There is no greater authority than His: no person, priest, church, religion, demon, or angel—not even Satan himself—can rival or threaten the incomprehensible authority of Jesus Christ.[124] He is above all that exists in the visible and the invisible world; He is above "names" (or beings) known to man as well as those unknown to us; only the Father Himself is exempt from submitting to Him (1 Cor. 15:27–28).

Christ's Supremacy over All Creation (1:22–23): "And He [God] put all things in subjection under His [Christ's] feet" (1:22a, bracketed words added)—the Creator put all Creation under the control of His Son. There is nothing that has been created—which includes all ungodly creatures as well as godly ones—that are not subject to Christ's authority. "Man's earthly dominion is only a shadow of Christ's universal dominion."[125]

"[A]nd gave Him as head over all things to the church" (1:22b): God, who made Christ as head over all things, also fittingly made Him as head of the church (Col. 1:18). Christ cannot be over all Creation without also being over the *new* creation, the body of believers (2 Cor. 5:17). This latter "creation" is unique and not interchangeable with the first creation. Scripture never refers to the physical Creation as the "body of Christ"; the entire physical Creation has not yet acknowledged Jesus as Lord, but this is a mandatory requirement of all who are "in Christ"; the church is incomplete without its head, and Christ's redemptive work is incomplete without a body of those redeemed; etc. Only in the spiritual body of Christ is "every spiritual blessing" found (recall 1:3); outside of this context is spiritual discord and alienation from God. The "fullness" of God which fills Christ also fills

---

124 Hendriksen believes that Paul may have had in mind those who indulged in angelology—angel worship and its attending doctrines—that was common in this region. "The names of angels, the various categories into which they were to be classified, and the worship due to them, seem to have been some of the topics on which the heretics concentrated their attention" (*NTC*, 101).

125 Lenski, *Interpretation*, 402.

His spiritual body (1:23; see Col. 1:19–20, 2:9–10). Just as God fills all of Creation, so His Son does the same (Eph. 4:6, Col. 1:15–17). Where God is, His Son and His Spirit must also be present: the Godhead, while three Personages, operates as "one"—a single entity (John 10:30, 17:22–23).

Section Two: Universal Salvation in Christ (2:1—3:21)

Salvation by Grace through Faith (Eph. 2:1–10)

The spiritual church of Christ is the sanctuary of redeemed souls who have submitted to Christ's pre-eminence over all Creation. This sanctuary could not have existed apart from Christ having ascended to the right hand of God; otherwise, He would not have had *authority* to build it. Once His divine *nature* (as the Son of God) and divine *mission* (as the Christ) had been established once and for all with irrefutable proofs, culminating in His own resurrection, then He could build a sanctuary for the redeemed of all time (see Mat. 16:18, John 20:31, etc.).

The State of the Lost (2:1–3): Prior to entering Christ's church, however, the sinful soul stood in a hopeless and wretched state of existence. "And you were dead" (2:1)—i.e., the soul was dead to *God* with regard to fellowship; God will not extend holy communion to that which is corrupted with sin and death.[126] In this "dead" state, the soul walked according to the "course of this world" (2:2)—what Jesus called the wide path "that leads to destruction" (Mat. 7:13). This "dead" soul was not literally unable to function or make decisions (as Calvinism assumes) but had chosen a route that would lead to its ultimate ruin rather than choosing to obey God.[127] Instead of giving allegiance to Christ, this "dead" soul gave allegiance to

---

126 Technically, the real cause of a soul's "death" is God's condemnation; sin is simply the agent of corruption, not an authority unto itself. Similarly, cancer does not kill people, but is an agent of corruption of the human body; the cancer-ridden body dies because of organ failure, not because of the mere presence of cancer. Since God is the sustainer of the human soul, when He withdraws His fellowship and condemns the sinful soul, it "dies" because of this absence of life, not because of the mere presence of sin. Sin is what causes God to withdraw spiritual life, and only He has the authority to do this; we cannot attribute this same authority to sin (or Satan).

127 This "deadness" also refers to allegiance. Just as the born-again believer is "dead to sin" (Rom. 6:11), he once was dead to God. Being "dead to sin" does not mean we are unconscious to temptations to sin, or that we cannot make decisions concerning sin; it means Christ is our new Master, and no longer sin.

another power: "the prince of the power of the air." This undeniably refers to Satan, "the god of this world" (2 Cor. 4:3–4). This description has several implications: first, Satan controls the realm (and thus the minds) of the ungodly; second, his power is derived from the earthly realm, not the spiritual; third, just as "air" is invisible and empty, so his activity is both invisible and spiritually empty (of anything good). It is his spirit or influence that drives the desires of unconverted souls; "the whole world lies in the power of the evil one" (1 John 5:19).[128]

Paul then switches to the first person to include himself (as a Jew) in the same lot as all Gentile sinners (2:3)—in essence, "We *all* used to live this way, to one extent or another. None of us were exempt." "Lusts" and "desires" of the flesh and mind refer to the carnal and ungodly passions and cravings that all people have who are uninfluenced by heavenly virtue. "Children of wrath" is set directly against "children of God" or "children of Light" (see 5:7–10). Those who live in opposition to God's will and God's Spirit incur the wrath and condemnation of God (Rom. 2:5–8, Gal. 5:16–21).

God's Grace through Christ (2:4–10): "But God" (2:4) implies: without God's mercy and intervention, we all would have succumbed to our deadened state of existence, having been destroyed by God's wrath against us. "Mercy" refers to the withholding of due punishment in anticipation of one's reform. God showed mercy to us sinners in anticipation of our salvation (2 Peter 3:9). God's "great love for us" is not what saves us; love alone cannot redeem our souls from condemnation. However, we are saved *because* of it: His love is the Great Cause or Prime Motive for all that God does for men; it is the impetus behind every aspect of redemption (see 1 John 4:7–10).

Thus, "even when we were dead … [He] made us alive" (2:5a)—this was

---

128 "Some have suggested that demons fill the literal air around us. Others suggest that Paul is playing on their supposed ideas of demons in the air and simply accommodating the ancient superstitions. It seems rather, that Paul is speaking of the existing moral atmosphere rather than the literal air we breathe. He is metaphorically saying that the Devil and his subordinates have causes human society to be so filled with their evil that to live among men is to breathe their evil. The prevailing mood or moral affinity of man is sinful and we are all surrounded by it. We formerly lived according to its dictates and died in it" (Caldwell, *Ephesians*, 71).

an act of love and mercy, but more directly it was an act of unfathomable *power*. The same power that raised Christ from His physical death also raises us from our spiritual "death"; this is the meaning of "together with Christ" (recall 1:19b–20; see Rom. 6:4–5).

"[B]y grace you have been saved" (2:5b)—lit. (in the Greek), "You are (in a continuous state of) having been saved by grace."[129] Grace includes all that God does to save the believer that he cannot do for himself. No one is saved apart from God's grace. (We must make a distinction here between saving grace and God's general kindness that He shows to all people. Simply because God blesses people does not save them from condemnation; He saves them only when they respond *rightly* to those blessings—see Rom. 2:4.) Only when He saves us by grace can He raise us up with Christ and seat us "in the heavenly places" (2:6)—i.e., not just in a manner *like* Christ's resurrection but also to the *place* where Christ was raised.

This latter statement has dual application. First, it has an immediate *spiritual* meaning, in that we are raised from our spiritual death; second, it anticipates our future *literal* (or bodily) resurrection in which we will be called forth from our physical grave, just as Christ came forth from His (John 5:28–29, Phil. 3:20–21, 1 Thess. 4:16, etc.).[130] In the spiritual body of Christ, we are already in communion with the Father. And while we have not yet *literally* been seated "in the heavenly places," we are promised that we will have a place there in the life to come (John 14:1–3, Rev. 3:21). "[S]o that in the ages to come He might show ... kindness" (2:7)—i.e., after we are with Him *in fact* and not merely through faith, God will show us visibly and personally all He had promised us when we first believed in Him. The recurring phrase "in Christ Jesus" determines the *context* in which mercy, grace, every spiritual blessing, and these promises are carried out. Those who are *not* "in Christ" are outside of these blessings since they remain outside of God's fellowship (cf. Rev. 22:14–15, in principle).

"For by grace you have been saved through faith" (2:8a)—a repeat of 2:5 but with renewed emphasis. The believer is saved because of what *God*

---

129 JFB, *Commentary* (electronic), on 2:5.
130 "Literal resurrection in the case of Jesus, spiritual in our case as pictured in baptism" (Robertson, *Word Pictures*, 524).

did (does); it is beyond the believer's ability to save himself. However, no one can *be* a believer who does not exercise obedient faith in the One who can save him.[131] Faith requires obedience for it to exist (or be made real). Divine grace is given because of human faith, never in the absence of it. No one is saved by grace *alone* anymore than he is saved by faith *alone*. While the act of salvation—raising a sinner from his death, walking him safely through this life, and ushering him into glory—requires incomprehensible power on God's part, He withholds this power from the one who does not demonstrate what He requires of him. God only approves of those who live by faith, not those who refuse this (Heb. 11:2, 10:36–39). In fact, people have *always* been saved by grace and through faith. While we now have far more knowledge than the ancients had (through better revelation and hindsight), the system of salvation has remained the same. The means of *redemption* also remains the same since all souls are redeemed by the blood of Christ.

While divine grace requires the presence of genuine faith, grace itself is "not of yourselves, it is the gift of God" (2:8b). ("It" here can refer to either "grace" or salvation; both references work.) This means we did not and cannot earn divine grace (Rom. 11:6); we are not worthy of it based upon personal merit; if God did not give us this gift, we could not have received it through any other means; and our salvation is fully dependent upon God and not human effort. Grace that is based upon works is no grace at all (2:9); it would be something *earned*, not a "gift" (Rom. 3:23–24, 4:3–5, 6:23, and Titus 3:4–7). People often boast about what they have accomplished; yet the Christian has no personal boast since his salvation depends upon what God has done for *him*, not what he has done for God (1 Cor. 1:30–31).

But our inability to save ourselves does not mean *nothing is required of us*. Paul emphasizes God's work; James (James 2:14–26) emphasizes the believer's work; both parts are necessary to bring about salvation. In fact, "we are His workmanship"—i.e., a personal handiwork; a masterpiece of God—"created in Christ Jesus for good works" (2:10). In essence, God has

---

131 However, not even human faith is self-generating. God gives us—through the proofs of His existence, His word, and the love which He has shown to us—*every reason to believe in Him*. Thus, while each person is responsible to *have* faith and to *exercise* it in obedience, God provides the basis *for* one's faith. Without God's part in this, not even human faith would be possible since we would have no good reason to have it.

made us a "new creation" (2 Cor. 5:17) for the purpose of producing good works in His name and for His glory (Mat. 5:16). Those who claim that we "do nothing" for our salvation do not understand (or will not accept) the necessary implications of this passage.[132] In saving us by grace, God expects us to walk (or live) by faith; this kind of life is impossible without works that befit our calling (see 4:1–3).

The "One New Man" in Christ (Eph. 2:11–22)

Those Separated from God (2:11–12): Paul now turns his attention specifically to the Gentiles, possibly to impress upon what God had done to bring them into a covenant relationship with Him (2:11). The Jews had already been a covenanted people and had enjoyed a special relationship with God in the past. But the Gentiles (as a group) remained a people alienated from God prior to the revelation of His gospel. Paul's message to them here is, in effect, "Remember from whence you came" or "Don't forget how spiritually hopeless you once were" (cf. 1 Cor. 1:25–31). The Jews regarded their circumcision as a badge of honor; it symbolized their special status with the Lord—and separated them from the "uncircumcised."[133] The Gentiles were considered "unclean" because of their uncircumcision—i.e., unfit for participation in any holy convocation or presentation before the Lord (Num. 19:20, etc.). Sadly, the Jews wrongly assumed that their circumcision equated to righteousness before God. They did not (or would not) understand that actions performed "by human hands" could not rectify spiritual deficiencies of the human soul.

Israelites were separated from God because of their sins (Isa. 59:1–2), but Gentiles were separated from Him because they were outside of a covenant of salvation altogether (2:12).[134] Being separated from all the privileges that

---

132 "Any theory which divorces the works a Christian must do from having any connection with his salvation is a false theory" (Coffman, *Commentary*, 164).

133 The "uncircumcised" were regarded as an unspiritual and morally unrefined people; see Gen. 34:14, Judg. 14:3, 1 Sam. 17:26, Isa. 52:1, etc. Thus, Jews did not regard themselves as merely *separated* from the Gentiles, but superior (morally, spiritually, and even culturally) to them. It is this condescension—and the natural indignant reciprocation of the Gentiles—that lay at the root of the Jew-Gentile animosity.

134 This does *not* mean that no Gentile could be saved who was not a proselyte to the

Israel enjoyed (see Rom. 9:4–5) put Gentiles at a great disadvantage in their understanding of God, His holy nature, spiritual enlightenment, moral conduct, and the afterlife. It was not as though Gentiles had no *opportunity* for such knowledge and insight but that they sought to gain such things through pagan beliefs and creature worship (Rom. 1:21–25). Thus, Paul provides a dark and miserable description of them:

- separated from those identified by the sign of the covenant (i.e., the Jews).
- excluded from the commonwealth of Israel (i.e., lacking citizenship).
- strangers to the covenants of promise (i.e., all the benefits and provisions God had made to those who were in fellowship with Him).
- having no hope—living in despair, never achieving spiritual freedom.
- without God— lit., godless (from Greek *atheos*, from which we get "atheists").

One "New Man" in Christ (2:13–18): "But now in Christ Jesus" (2:13)— i.e., the situation has been radically changed: Jews and Gentiles are now given equal opportunity to have fellowship with God; no person or ethnic group has an advantage over another with respect to salvation.[135] What brought the Gentile "near" to God was not the Jews, nor circumcision, but the blood of Christ. This blood serves as the unifying agent for all men: "all have sinned" (Rom. 3:23) and therefore all need redemption; no one is redeemed except through the blood of Christ (recall 1:7). Both groups are united *not* by religion, "church," or common beliefs. Christ Himself is who unites all people in His church—a fact which Christians today must never lose sight of. All believers have peace with God only because Christ has *become* our Peace (2:14). "Both groups" refers to Jews and Gentiles; but

---

Jewish religion. Paul is speaking in general terms about *all* Gentiles (i.e., of a multitude of nations), not what happened in every case. As we have already learned, *any* man could be saved by divine grace through the exercise of human faith. Thus, even a Gentile who had nothing to do with the Israelite covenant could find favor with God if he lived by faith in what he *did* know about Him (Rom. 2:12–16, 25–29).

135 Jews considered themselves "close" to God because of the special status they enjoyed with Him through covenant; thus, from their perspective, Gentiles were "far off." What the Jews failed to consider was the fact that their Jewish ethnicity was determined by God, not by their personal choice or merit. For an excellent foreshadow of God's universal salvation, see Isa. 49:6 and 55:1–7.

in Christ, earthly statuses and ethnicities lose all distinction: He has made them both into "one."[136]

The "barrier of the dividing wall [or, middle wall of partition]" (2:14) alludes to the wall in the Jewish temple area that separated the Court of the Gentiles from the sacred areas that only Jews could access (Acts 21:28–29). In Paul's day, a sign was placed upon this wall that promised execution to any Gentile who transgressed this barrier.[137] This wall symbolized the separation of Jews from Gentiles: even when a Gentile became a proselyte to the Jewish religion, he was still regarded as a *Gentile*—a second-class citizen in the Jews' eyes.

When Paul wrote these words, Christ had not taken down the wall in the temple area—yet. (He did prophesy, however, that a foreign army would dismantle the entire temple *and* its walls, underscoring the obsolescence of these structures; see Mat. 24:1–2, Luke 19:41–44, etc.) But He did remove a far greater barrier wall—not what merely separated Jew and Gentile but what separated *all* men from *Himself* because of human sin. Even though the Jew could enter the inner courts of the temple, he still could not enter the innermost sanctuary of the temple (the "Holy of Holies"), which illustrated his own separation from the holiness of God. In essence, all that separated men *from other men* as well as whatever separated men *from God*, Christ took away (or abolished) in His single act of supreme sacrifice on the cross (2:15). The destruction of this (symbolic) "wall" removed the enmity between men and God; it also removed ("in Christ") the enmity between men.

"Enmity" means hostility (that creates enemies), animosity, or hatred. Here (2:15) it refers to what the Law of Moses itself represented: the Law separated Jews from Gentiles, *and* it separated *all* men from God (since no

---

136 "Both Jewish and Gentile Christians needed to be reminded that they were saved by grace. It was necessary for them to remember their former state of hardened hearts and sinful lusts in order to produce humility, penitence, gratitude, and love for God. The man does not have peace within himself if he find himself Christless, stateless, homeless, hopeless, and Godless. Only the Lord Jesus Christ can offer inner peace by providing that which man lacks in his soul" (Caldwell, *Ephesians*, 94).

137 The plaque read (translated): "No foreigner may enter within the barricade which surrounds the sanctuary and enclosure. Anyone who is caught doing so will have himself to blame for his ensuing death" (Hendriksen, *NTC*, 133).

man could keep its ordinances entirely, regardless of his ethnicity). The Law could not heal or forgive sinners; it could only condemn them. Likewise, the Law could not bridge gaps or unite men but only perpetuated the separation between them. The only way to bring men together as "one" *and* bring this "one new man" into fellowship with God was to remove the condemnation of Law—the "wall" that kept everyone distinctly separated.[138] And the only way to remove the condemnation of Law was to *fulfill* the Law, thus completing its purpose and satisfying the One who gave it. This is what Christ did with His perfect life and through His perfect sacrifice: He fulfilled the Law entirely, allowing for a *new* covenant and (thus) a *new* law to take its place. In so doing, He united all men *in Himself*—as one new body of believers—and He personally represents that body *as Himself* before the Father (2:16). Thus, the "reconciliation" is threefold: He has reconciled the two groups into one; He has reconciled believers from either covenant into one sanctuary; and He has reconciled this sanctified group with the Father (see 2 Cor. 5:18–20, Rom. 5:10, Gal. 3:28, Col. 1:19–20, and 3:15).

Jesus "preached peace" in that He proclaimed a means by which men could enjoy fellowship with God *and* each other (2:17; see Isa. 57:19–21, John 14:27, and 16:33).[139] "No man can be in union with God without being in union and fellowship with every other being in the universe in union with Him."[140] Those who are "far away" refer to the Gentiles; those who are "near" refer to the Jews. "[F]or through Him we both have our access in one Spirit to the Father" (2:18)—our "access [or, admission; introduction]" is *through* Christ and *in* the Holy Spirit. Christ has paved the way with His blood; He

---

138 To say that the *Law* was the enmity or point of separation may be misleading if taken out of context. The Law itself did not create hatred or enmity; rather, it was men's failure to *keep* God's laws that creates this. Such failure brought about condemnation; condemnation brings about death (see 1 Cor. 15:56). Specifically, then, the enmity is not the Law itself, but the condemnation brought about *because* of the Law—a condemnation which was the result of sin, not legal commandments.

139 Actually, He also preached that His gospel would create division and conflict among men. The gospel itself is not divided, nor is it divisive to those who believe in God; but it would separate such people from those who resisted it (Mat. 10:34, Luke 12:41). The "peace" He preached, then, was solely to those who would surrender to the terms and conditions *of* that peace. In my opinion, it is this union of two formerly hostile and incompatible people into "one new man" that fulfills the spiritual prophecy of Isa. 11:5–9.

140 David Lipscomb, *A Commentary on the New Testament Epistles, volume IV: Ephesians, Philippians and Colossians* (Nashville: Gospel Advocate Co., 1976), 49.

has entered the heavenly tabernacle with Himself as the once-for-all sacrifice on our behalf (Heb. 9:11–12). Christ built His church and infused it with His blood; the Holy Spirit breathed life into this body and made it a living organism (cf. Gen. 2:7). Christ deals with the sins of men by providing *atonement* for men's souls; the Spirit deals with sanctifying and consecrating these same souls for service in the kingdom (1 Peter 1:2). Christ and the Holy Spirit work together to prepare men to enter *fellowship* with God. Through *one* Savior, condemnation (for sin) is removed; in *one* Spirit, those redeemed are added into *one* body by "one baptism" (see 1 Cor. 12:12–13, Eph. 4:5). The result is that Christians everywhere become "one new man" (recall 2:15). This removes any need for an intercessory priesthood since Christ is our High Priest (Heb. 4:14–16) and we pray directly to God in the Spirit (see Rom. 8:26–27, Eph. 6:18, and Jude 1:20).

The Spiritual Temple of God (2:19–22): "So then" (2:19)—i.e., since these things are true, the following is also true. "Strangers" are set in contrast to members of the "household of God"; "aliens" are set against "fellow citizens with the saints" (cf. Phil. 3:20). The status of the believing Gentile has changed completely; whatever had been denied him before is now his in abundance. Paul may have intentionally used architectural "temple" imagery as a sharp contrast to the temple of Diana [Artemis] that was the pride of the unconverted Ephesians (see "Introduction"). That temple was a man-made, physical structure; it was subject to all the ravages of time, the elements, natural calamity (such as earthquakes), and human destruction: just as men had assembled it, so men could disassemble it. The holy temple of God (the church), however:

- is spiritual in nature—it is "not of this world" (John 18:36).
- is divinely created, divinely owned, and divinely operated.
- is immune to earthly ravages or destruction—it cannot deteriorate or be destroyed.
- is untouched by those who would oppose it—it is unassailable to its enemies.
- is indissoluble—it is permanent and eternal in nature.
- does not rest upon an earthly foundation but an omnipotent Divine Being (1 Cor. 3:11) whose message has been accurately and successfully communicated to the world through His own prophets and apostles

(2:20; see Acts 3:19–25 and Col. 1:23b).
- has a "cornerstone"—the most critical component of the foundation by which the entire structure is oriented—as a fulfillment of divine prophecy (Psalm 118:22, Isa. 28:16, Acts 4:11–12, and 1 Peter 2:6–7).[141] This determines not only the stability and solidity of the structure but—in the prophetic application to Christ's church—also its nature, character, and direction (or purpose).
- is both built and held together by the same power with which Christ keeps all of Creation intact (Col. 1:16–18).
- is *growing*—it is not a lifeless, inanimate structure but a living organism that pulses with the blood of Christ and breathes with the Spirit of God.
- is the accumulation of living souls that are "being built together" into one completely unified, perfectly organized, and fully functional *body* (2:22).
- is a "dwelling of God in the Spirit"—it serves as a temple in which God dwells. Wherever God is (or dwells), His Spirit is also; if we have fellowship with God, we have fellowship with His Spirit also (2 Cor. 13:14).[142] It is the Holy Spirit's sanctifying and consecratory work that *makes possible* the Father's presence.

The context in this passage (2:13–22) is universal in scope. It does not deal with an individual believer, congregations of believers, or the church at Ephesus specifically; it deals solely and especially with the *entire body* of believers. The "one new man" is the entire body of Christ—the assembly of human souls redeemed by the blood of Christ. This assembly includes faithful believers still living on earth as well as those who have already died in the Lord. It includes those saved by grace through faith in earlier times as well as those whose fellowship with God is defined through the revealed gospel of Christ. While principles from this passage may apply on a smaller level—e.g., God indwells the individual believer as He does the entire

---

141 See Lenski's comments (*Interpretation*, 454–455) for valuable insight into the "cornerstone" concept.

142 Some commentators want "in the Spirit" to read "in the spirit"—i.e., in man's spirit (JFB, *Commentary* [electronic], on 2:22). This is unacceptable, given the context. While it is true that God communes with our spirit, the context here is not dealing with how God communes with an individual believer, but how *the body of Christ* communes with *God the Father*. Thus, "in the Spirit" can only mean, in essence, "by the indwelling of God's Holy Spirit in the church."

church (Rom. 8:9)—we should not ignore the primary context in which these words were written.

Paul's Ministry to the Revealed Gospel (Eph. 3:1–13)

"For this reason" (3:1) builds upon what has been said: since Jews and Gentiles are made "one new man" in Christ, Paul's original purpose here is to offer a prayer on behalf of both groups within the church at Ephesus. Yet, he has suffered imprisonment for having preached this message of universal salvation, and it may be this very thought that causes him to digress into a further explanation on this subject. Thus, what he begins in 3:1 is abruptly postponed until 3:14 when he resumes his original intention. Paul hints at a second purpose in 3:13: some of the Ephesian Christians may have thought that Paul's imprisonment has undermined the effect or credibility of the gospel. Not only this, but Paul's enemies cited his imprisonment as a kind of "proof" that he was a fraud. "It is not improbable that these opponents viewed his very *imprisonment* as a sign of the falsity of his pretentions. So, instead of carefully avoiding this subject he starts right out by boldly calling attention to it."[143]

The "Mystery" Revealed (3:2–10): Earlier in the letter, Paul had mentioned the "mystery of [God's] will" (1:9) but now wishes to expound upon that mystery to impress upon the Ephesians its importance (3:2–3). The stewardship that God entrusted to Paul (1 Cor. 4:1, Col. 1:25–27) included divine revelations concerning His unfolding plan of salvation to all humanity. While this message was once mysterious and obscured in the prophets (see Isa. 49:5–6, for example), it has now been fully revealed through Christ and His apostles, being confirmed by miraculous proofs of its genuineness (Gal. 1:11–12, Heb. 2:3–4, etc.).

Now that this mystery has been revealed—and has become a permanent historical record—believers can "read" and "understand" what God had longed to unveil all along (3:4–5). "If God did not wish to reveal his mind in such a way that man can understand, there was no point in giving the Bible

---

[143] Hendriksen, *NTC*, 150; emphasis is his.

at all."[144] In other words, Paul is not trying to keep anything secret but *expects* the Ephesians (and all believers) to study and become enlightened through that which the Holy Spirit has disclosed to him.[145] The phrase "in the Spirit" (3:5) indicates the method of disclosure: whether it was the OT prophets, prophets within the church, or Christ's own apostles, each minister received his information directly from the Holy Spirit by way of divine revelation (2 Peter 3:1–2). While many men received such revelations over an extended period, the result is one grand mystery that culminates in what we know as the gospel of Christ.

Having been very general in his comments so far, Paul is now more specific (3:6). The "mystery" refers to salvation through Jesus Christ to which He invites *all* people through the proclamation of the gospel. In this universal salvation, there is no partiality (Rom. 2:9–11); no one will be disappointed or put to shame (Rom. 10:11–13); no one "in Christ" will be a second-class citizen to anyone else in the church. "The mystery was not that the Gentiles should be saved—there is much in the OT concerning that, particularly in Isaiah—but that they should be joined with Jews in one body!"[146] While today the idea of a universal salvation might seem unremarkable, in Paul's day it was a radical and revolutionary idea that was as astonishing to Gentiles as it was to Jews. In Christ's church, then, Gentiles and Jews are:

- ❏ **fellow heirs.** Since *all* believers are "sons of God through faith" by adoption (Gal. 3:26, 4:4–7), no "son" has an advantage over another regarding inheritance. In Christ, *all* are heirs of the promises of God (Gal. 3:29), just as *all* have fallen short of the glory of God and need the same kind of redemption. While sin makes all men equally condemnable, grace makes all men equally righteous.
- ❏ **fellow members of the body of Christ.** This does not mean that every member has equal responsibilities or gifts (Rom. 12:4–8, 1 Cor. 12:29–30, Eph. 4:7, etc.); it *does* mean that every member has an important and functional role within the body (1 Cor. 12:14–19). Jewish Christians, then, are not superior members over Gentile believers; Gentile

---

144 Caldwell, *Ephesians*, 109.

145 There are exceptions to this, as indicated in 2 Cor. 12:1–4, but these are dictated by God, not Paul.

146 Alfred Martin, as quoted in Coffman, *Commentary*, 184.

Christians are not inferior to their Jewish brethren. The underlying implication here is that of *wholeness* and *completion*: only a whole and completely intact "body" can serve God (cf. Lev. 21:16–23, in principle). In essence, Christ's "body" (His church) is made complete now that *all* people have been invited into it.

- **fellow partakers of the promise in Christ Jesus.** A "partaker" is literally a co-participant or joint-sharer (in something).[147] The ancient Jews prided themselves on being the sole recipients of the Law, temple, priesthood, and sacrificial system; in their minds, this made them more important (to God) than their heathen counterparts—even those heathens who had converted to the Jewish religion. Yet Paul's declaration here shatters all such misconceptions and presumptions. God is no respecter of persons (Acts 10:34–35) and has provided opportunity for *all* men to partake of His saving grace. Now, both Jew and Gentile work shoulder-to-shoulder in the kingdom of God; both serve the same Master; and both look forward to the same future glory.

The "gift of God's grace" (3:7) given to Paul does not refer to a measure of *salvation*—Paul was not more "saved" than any other believer—but rather to the level of responsibility entrusted to him. (One only needs to read the parable of the talents to understand this concept—Mat. 25:14–30.) In either case, whether regarding salvation or one's personal ministry, God is the *Giver* of such things, and these are all "gifts" that cannot be earned or merited. "[A]ccording to the working of His power" gives God full credit for what Paul has accomplished in Christ's name (see Phil. 2:13 and Col. 1:29). Paul refers to himself *personally* as "the very least of all saints" (3:8) because of the great violence and harm that he once brought upon the church (see Acts 26:9–11, 1 Tim. 1:12–16). Even so, he does not consider his *ministry* or his *apostolic authority* in this way but views these endowments with the highest regard (2 Cor. 11:5). The "unfathomable [or, untraceable; unsearchable] riches in Christ" is not a mere decorative phrase but speaks to the unlimited *wealth* and *power* which Christ possesses as the King over God's kingdom. With such incomprehensible resources, He leads His church not only safely through this life; He can preserve it in the life to come. The "administration

---

147 Often, "partaker" comes from the same Greek word (*koinonos* or *koinonia*) meaning also "(a) sharing," "fellowship," or "communion." Here, however, the Greek word is *summetochos*, which is also used in 5:6–7.

of the mystery ... made known through the church" (3:9–10) reminds us of what Paul has already said about Christ (recall 1:9–10).

While Christ is the summing up of all things, His *church* is the group which proclaims Him to the world, being the "pillar and support of the truth" of what the Spirit has revealed (1 Tim. 3:14–16). "[T]he rulers and authorities in the heavenly {places}" (3:10) remains an obscure reference; our best approach to such references is to seek the most *natural* and *simplest* answer rather than speculate about things beyond our knowledge. Such "rulers and authorities" refers to angels and other heavenly beings who themselves have waited to see the unveiling of God's plan of redemption (cf. 1 Peter 1:10–12). Angels are ministers *to* the saints and are not always the first to receive what God intended *for* the saints (Heb. 1:14).

God's "Eternal Purpose" (3:11–12): "{This was} in accordance with the eternal purpose" (3:11)—referring to the administration of the unfolding mystery of the gospel of which Paul just spoke. God's design to bring salvation to all humankind through His Son, Jesus Christ, has been in His mind (or, has been His plan) since before He laid the foundations of the earth.[148] In Christ, we have "boldness [or, cheerful assurance]" and "confident access" to God (3:12; see Heb. 10:19–22).[149] Christ presents us before the Father since we, having sinned against Him, are unable to present ourselves before Him without Christ's advocacy. To *prepare* us for this presentation, He must first cleanse us of our sins, then consecrate us for holy service. While this process involves both Christ *and* the Holy Spirit (recall 2:18), it is Christ who makes this possible through His blood (i.e., His once-for-all offering as an atonement for our sin).

Paul summarizes this lengthy parenthetical, which began in 3:2, with an encouragement to the Ephesians (3:13). Since the gospel plan is an "eternal purpose" finished by God's own Son, the imprisonment of one of its

---

148 There is, by necessity, "overtones of the pre-existence and godhead of the Lord Jesus Christ in this declaration" (Coffman, *Commentary*, 188).

149 "Boldness [*parresian*] is translated from a combination of two words which mean 'all-telling' (*pas*, all; and *rhesis*, a speech). It points to boldness in speaking, freedom of speech, frankness and absence of fear or shame in unreserved openness" (Caldwell, *Ephesians*, 124). It is also translated in the NT as "publicly," "openly," "plainly," and "confidently (or confidence)."

spokesmen is not going to threaten its effectiveness (see 2 Tim. 2:8–9). On the contrary, Paul's sufferings have emboldened the saints and have helped to spread the word of Christ further than it would have been otherwise (see Phil. 1:12–14).

Paul's Second Prayer for the Ephesians (Eph. 3:14–21)

"For this reason" (3:14)—a return to what he began in 3:1, but also a continuation of what has been developed in 3:2–13. Paul assumes a submissive physical posture ("I bow my knees") in presenting this prayer to God on behalf of the Ephesians and, in effect, saints everywhere.[150] While we cannot use such passages to impose this posture upon all who pray, there are sufficient references in Scripture to support this as a sign of reverence and voluntary submission to one who is higher in authority:

- "And a leper came to Him and bowed down before Him, and said, 'Lord, if You are willing, You can make me clean'" (Mat. 8:2).
- "While He was saying these things to them, a synagogue official [Jairus] came and bowed down before Him, and said, 'My daughter has just died; but come and lay Your hand on her, and she will live'" (Mat. 9:18).
- "Then the mother of the sons of Zebedee came to Jesus with her sons, bowing down and making a request of Him" (Mat. 20:20).
- "Seeing Jesus from a distance, he ran up and bowed down before Him" (Mark 5:6). This passage is particularly remarkable because it is a *demon-possessed man* who does this. Even the demons know to bow in the presence of God's Son.
- "But after hearing of Him, a woman whose little daughter had an unclean spirit immediately came and fell at His feet" (Mark 7:25).
- "But when Simon Peter saw that, he fell down at Jesus' feet, saying, 'Go away from me Lord, for I am a sinful man, O Lord!'" (Luke 5:8).

---

150 "To bow [*kampto*, to bend] the knees [*gonata*] is one of those great symbols of earnest, deep emotion associated with prayer. Solemn, deliberate humility is important for proper communion with God. In bowing down, the one beseeching God's favor recognizes his own weaknesses and subjects himself to God. It should never be done ostentatiously, displaying oneself to be seen of men. Care should be taken to avoid mock humility and situations which distract others because we are 'getting ourselves in a position to pray'" (Caldwell, *Ephesians*, 130).

- "Now one of them, when he saw that he had been healed, turned back, glorifying God with a loud voice, and he fell on his face at His feet, giving thanks to Him. And he was a Samaritan" (Luke 17:15–16).
- "Therefore, when Mary came where Jesus was, she saw Him, and fell at His feet, saying to Him, 'Lord, if You had been here, my brother would not have died'" (John 11:32).
- "But what is the divine response to him? 'I have kept for Myself seven thousand men who have not bowed the knee to Baal'" (Rom. 11:4). This passage shows the opposite effect: those who bow in reverence to God must not bow to any other god.
- "For this reason also, God highly exalted Him, and bestowed on Him the name which is above every name, so that at the name of Jesus every knee will bow, of those who are in heaven and on earth and under the earth, and that every tongue will confess that Jesus Christ is Lord, to the glory of God the Father" (Phil. 2:9–11).

The point is clear: it is *most appropriate* to bow one's knees—or one's entire body—in coming before the "throne of grace" (Heb. 4:16). "The bodily attitude during prayer is important, for it reflects the soul's attitude toward God."[151]

Paul continues his prayer, praising God as the authority ("Father") for "every 'family'" in heaven and on earth (3:15). We are not to press this thought too literally: we have no indication that there are angelic "families" in heaven like our human families on earth (i.e., that engage in marriage and procreation). "Family" can have a much broader connotation than an ancestral lineage; it can also refer to a group of people, related families, or nations. In a general sense, it can refer to a particular class or strata of living creatures (such as a genus or species of animals). Thus, "families" in heaven may simply refer to the different classes or designations of angelic beings, as we see described (albeit in a visionary context) in *Revelation*. Regardless, the supreme or overarching idea here is that *every living being* or *group of beings* derives its power, authority, and existence from the Father (1 Cor. 8:5). In a real sense, we—people, angels, and all heavenly creatures—are one *great* "family" because we are all created beings, and all have the same Creator.

---

151 Lenski, *Interpretation*, 489.

The Indwelling of Christ in the Believer (3:16–19): Through His sovereign power, infinite wealth, and incalculable resources, God the Father grants "riches" to those who belong to Him (3:16). This is not material wealth, but something far greater: spiritual blessings (1:3), acts of divine grace (2:8), confident access to the throne of God (3:12), and a heavenly inheritance (1:13–14). Paul often prays for God to impart divine "strength" to believers, since our human strength is limited in ability, endurance, and perspective (Col. 1:11, 2 Thess. 3:3, etc.). This "power" which strengthens the believer comes through God's Spirit which indwells him in his "inner man"—i.e., in a spiritual manner, not a literal or physical one. Paul is not referring here to *miraculous gifts*: the context has not even mentioned them; they cannot be necessarily implied; and what he says here applies to all Christians. This "power" is that which strengthens, renews (2 Cor. 4:18), and generates "fruit" (Gal. 5:22–23, Col. 1:9–10). The believer depends upon God to do for him what he cannot do for himself, not what he is capable of doing on his own. This is as true in his everyday walk with the Spirit (Gal. 5:16–17) as it is regarding his ultimate salvation.

"So that Christ may dwell in your hearts through faith" (3:17)—not literally (any more than sin literally dwells in an unbeliever's heart) but an indwelling that is *real* and *effective* all the same. This indwelling (or abiding presence) includes the internalization of His words (John 15:7) but is not limited to mere words or human knowledge of God. It also refers to His love (1 John 4:16), His attitude (Phil. 2:5), His peace (Rom. 5:1–2), His gospel (Col. 3:15–16), and His Spirit (Rom. 8:9). Jesus said, "Apart from Me, you can do nothing" (John 15:5): without His power working within us, we are incapable of overcoming our own weaknesses and limitations.

We cannot think that by merely reading the words of Scripture, somehow—without a miracle being performed!—we will be divinely strengthened. On the other hand, "It is very hurtful for one to think that he can receive the help of the Spirit without taking the word of the Spirit into the heart."[152] Scripture teaches us what to believe, how to believe, and in whom to believe; yet words on a page cannot equal or replace what Christ alone does by indwelling the believer's heart. Christ and His love abiding in the heart of the believer provides the stability, strength, and constancy he needs to overcome this

---
152 Lipscomb, *Commentary*, 63.

world (John 16:33). As a result, the believer will be "rooted and grounded in love"—he will be solid, immovable, and enduring, "like a tree firmly planted by streams of water" (Psalm 1:3). "The strengthening of faith and of love is to fill us with the knowledge of the divine reality on which all our faith and our love rest."[153]

With the presence of Christ in his heart, and his having been immersed in God's love, the believer has his spiritual "eyes" opened to see far more than at first. Together with like-minded believers, he will be able to "comprehend [or, grasp]" all the different *dimensions* of this love—its breadth, length, height, and depth (3:18).[154] God's love is not a one-track, linear concept; it is not a monochrome picture. Instead, it is a manifold and variegated mosaic that extends in every direction beyond what the human mind can conceive. This love "surpasses knowledge" (3:19)—i.e., it exceeds human measurement; it goes far beyond rational explanation; it is not a mere subject that one studies (like math, science, or history). Paul is not describing a mere feeling or emotion here. God's love is real, practical, and personal: since God *is* love (1 John 4:8), whenever we discuss the love *of* God, we refer to who God *is* (His essential nature). "[T]hat you … the fullness of God" is an ideal objective—something toward which "all the saints" are ever-nearing. ("You" here is a collective pronoun, meaning "all of you.") Christ's *church* is filled with God's "fullness," just as Jesus Himself was filled with this fullness while He fulfilled His ministry to the Father (Col. 1:19, 2:9–10).

A Hymn of Praise (3:20–21): Paul fittingly ends his prayer with a doxology (or hymn of praise)—an appropriate conclusion to the transcendent message of God's gospel (3:20–21). It is natural (and human) for people to be limited in their spiritual thinking; as a result, they limit their understanding of God's power and capability. Paul shatters such human perspectives: "[God] is able to do far more abundantly beyond all that we ask or think."[155] God already proved this through the record of Scripture.

---

153 Lenski, *Interpretation*, 496.

154 Paul did not supply a prepositional phrase that we would normally expect to follow these nouns (breadth, length, height, depth). The meaning, however, seems clear enough: he speaks of "love" directly before and after these words, so that their association is unmistakable.

155 "This is another one of Paul's super-superlatives, coined to express God's capacity to transcend all that we ask or think" (F. F. Bruce, as quoted in Coffman, *Commentary*, 194).

Also, by virtue of His own sovereign will, omniscience, and absolute power, He cannot be limited or constrained by human thinking. While many people are imprisoned by their own expectations, circumstances, or understanding, God is not limited by anyone or anything. He does not give only *what* we ask for, but even *more* than we ever thought to request of Him. He is not what (or who) we *think* He is, He is already far beyond what we could ever *imagine* Him to be.

"[T]he power that works within us" is not ours but God's, which performs beyond what we are able to on our own. Otherwise, we would not need Him to impart anything to us, and it would be redundant to pray *for* power or strength that we already possess. Instead, this "power" is that of Christ and the Holy Spirit working in the heart of the believer to sanctify, strengthen, transform, and perfect him (2 Cor. 12:9, James 1:5–7, and 1 Peter 5:10). "[T]o Him be the glory" (3:21)—i.e., God's sovereign greatness is displayed in the body of believers (the church) as well as in His own Son. His glory is timeless and changeless ("forever and ever"), just as God and His Son are timeless and changeless (Psalm 45:17, 72:17, Heb. 13:8, and Rev. 5:13).

SECTION THREE:
THE UNITY OF CHRIST'S BODY
(4:1–16)

The Unity of the Spirit
(Eph. 4:1–6)

The Unity of the Spirit (4:1–3): Having expounded upon the essential *theology* upon which Christ has established His church, Paul now transitions to the *practical application* of this exposition. Once again, he makes an appeal to the Ephesian Christians as one imprisoned for the cause of Christ (4:1; recall 3:1): "I ... implore you"—lit., I beg or beseech you; I ask that you strongly consider (this). "[W]alk in a manner worthy of the calling ... called"—i.e., live according to the holy way in which Christ called you through His gospel. He calls us in love, truth, and purity; there is no hypocrisy, deceit, or false promises in His message. As He has called us, so we are to live; as He has committed Himself to us, so we are to commit ourselves to Him. Paul then explains more of what he means by this "manner" (4:2–3):

- **"with all humility"**—or, with a humble spirit or lowliness. The humble person defers to others and regards them as more important than himself. Many people wrongly see humility as a sign of weakness; instead, it is a masterful control of one's own emotions, will, human pride. God reveals it as a necessary means to greatness (Mat. 20:26–27, 1 Peter 5:5–6).
- **"gentleness"**—or, meekness or mild-mannered-ness. This characteristic is often directly associated with humility, since it defines the outward behavior of the one who is humble. It is also a common disposition of those conditioned by Christ (Mat. 11:29, Phil. 4:5, Titus 3:1–2, etc.).[156]
- **"patience"**—or, longsuffering. Patience refers to the willingness to wait,

---

[156] "Meekness has two frames of reference: toward God and toward our fellow man. Meekness toward God is the disposition which moves us to accept his word as right and his dealings with us as just and good. ... Gentleness toward our fellow man grows out of our meekness toward God. It involves willingness to suffer wrong without retaliation. It involves a mild and forgiving spirit of gentleness as opposed to harsh rebellion and/or violence" (Caldwell, *Ephesians*, 157).

despite a person's stubbornness or immaturity, in anticipation of his reformed attitude or behavior. This is how Christians are to deal with one another, just as God shows great patience toward us (Rom. 2:4, 2 Peter 3:9).

- **"showing tolerance for one another"**—or, being forbearing, and forgiving as needed. We might illustrate tolerance with the pistons in an internal-combustion engine: for the pistons to function, they need to have enough *tolerance* or *clearance* to move—not too much, but not too little, either. So it is with our dealings with people: we cannot allow them to do anything they want (i.e., carelessly engage in sinful behavior), but we must give them enough space or clearance to make mistakes and *be human* without leveling condemnation against them for every error in judgment (Col. 3:12–13).
- **"being diligent to preserve the unity of the Spirit in the bond of peace."** The "unity of the Spirit" cannot mean that which binds the *Godhead* together but what binds *Christians* to God and each other. It is the Spirit-revealed "message of truth, the gospel of your salvation" (recall 1:13) that defines our fellowship with God. "Unequivocally, biblical unity on any question about which God has spoken must be based upon what God says."[157] Wherever is unity must also be peace, and vice versa. God-given peace binds fellow believers together in the Spirit; at the same time, to enjoy that peace, believers must be united in what they *believe* and *teach* (1 Cor. 4:17). They must be diligent to preserve this unity since it cannot happen by accident and will not be sustained on autopilot.

The Doctrine of the Spirit (4:4–6): At this point, someone might ask, "What exactly *defines* the 'unity of the Spirit' in our beliefs and teaching?" Paul immediately answers this (4:4–6). The oneness of the body of Christ mirrors the oneness of its doctrine. A variety of conflicting and contradictory doctrines cannot achieve unity or peace; likewise, a multiplicity of different "faiths" defined by man-made religions (i.e., denominationalism, sectarianism, and all other forms of religious division) cannot possibly support the unity of God's Holy Spirit. Conformity to the gospel of Christ produces unity with the Spirit, as well as unity *of* the Spirit among fellow

---

157 *Ibid.*, 161.

believers.[158] The church's unifying doctrine is not *limited* to the seven points given here by Paul, but it cannot fail to *embrace* them, either. In other words, if any person claims to be a Christian, he must believe and teach *at least* these things:

- **One body.** The only "body" thus far identified in *Ephesians* has been the body of Christ; we have no reason to introduce a different "body" here. All believers are brought together into *one* body, not many. While many separate congregations of believers are possible, it is impossible to have many separate *bodies of Christ*. Just as Christ Himself is not divided, so His church is not divided (1 Cor. 1:13). Again, the conception of one head (Christ) and many bodies (all claiming "unity" with Christ) is incompatible with this doctrine. God has given authority for only *one* church to exist: that which His Son has built—the spiritual body of believers redeemed by His blood in response to their "obedience of faith" (Rom. 16:25–26).
- **One Spirit.** Christ is the head of His body; but the body of Christ is filled with the Spirit of God. Through the Spirit, the body is *united* rather than being a fractured mass of confusion (which does not conform to God's "eternal purpose"—recall 3:11). Christians are not bound by a common religion but by a common Spirit who has instructed us what to believe and how to conduct ourselves (1 Cor. 12:13). The unity of the doctrine of the church must conform exactly to the united doctrine that He has revealed. If indeed we wish to be Christians, this cannot be otherwise.
- **One hope.** Since believers are united in *one body* by *one Spirit*, it naturally follows that they all share *one hope*—that is, an anticipation of future glory guaranteed by the Spirit who indwells each believer (Eph. 1:13–14, 1 Peter 1:3–5). There is no tiered system or a clergy-laity division in the church; we are all equals as brothers and sisters in Christ. No one's "calling" is superior to anyone else's. We have not been "called" by several different gospels or by several different "spirits" but by one gospel and one Spirit. Thus, our "calling" is singular in design and united in objective, conforming to the One who called us.

---

158 For further study on the gospel pattern and the Holy Spirit's work within Christ's church, I strongly recommend two of my books: *The Holy Spirit: A Biblical Perspective* (2010) and *The New Testament Pattern: God's Plan for Christians and Their Churches* (2023); go to www.spiritbuilding.com/chad.

- **One Lord.** The context demands that "Lord" here refers to Christ, since the Spirit has already been mentioned and the Father will be mentioned shortly. The church does not submit to many "lords" but to one; we do not speak with many authorities (as from many different men) but with one authority—that of the Lord Jesus Christ. If we call Jesus "Lord," then we must do what He commands us through His word (Mat. 7:21, Luke 6:46, and John 14:15).
- **One faith.** One commentary claims, "Faith here is not *what we believe, but rather the act of* believing."[159] This does not seem at all to be the case here. Paul is not talking about an act of believing; he is specifically defining some of the core teachings that *must be believed*. Thus, "one faith" is that one *gospel message* which a person must believe, not one's personal belief system. Again, the denominational concept of one body filled with many different doctrines or teachings of faith is incompatible with this doctrine.[160] The existence of many *congregations* of God's people is supported by Scripture; the teaching of many *religions* is not.
- **One baptism.** Christ requires that believers both *do* and *teach* this "one baptism." This is not a baptism with the Holy Spirit (as some assume). The only baptism God requires of believers in order "to preserve the unity of the Spirit" (4:3) is immersion in water. This symbolic death, burial, and resurrection process compares to Christ's own literal death, burial, and resurrection. Through this symbolic act, we are "united with {Him} in the likeness of His death" (Rom. 6:5) and are "clothed" with Christ (Gal. 3:27).[161] Thus, the acceptance of *one Lord* leads the believer to His *one system of faith*, which necessarily requires this *one baptism* as a

---

159 JFB, *Commentary* (electronic), on 4:5; emphasis is theirs.

160 The denominationalist will argue, "Christ is 'one vine' with many 'branches,'" referring to John 15:1–6. Thus, he will assume that each "branch" is a different denomination or "Christian faith." Yet Jesus was talking about *individual believers* as "branches," not conflicting religions. Furthermore, Jesus and His apostles have only taught *one* faith, not many.

161 Some commentators are puzzled by the omission of the "other" sacrament, the Lord's Supper. Thus, they assume that this baptism must be a "Spirit baptism" rather than literal or water baptism. Such reasoning is unnecessary and presumptive. Paul is speaking about the foundational doctrine of our unity *with* the Spirit—i.e., what we must believe and what we must have done to conform to His revealed Word. Just as the Lord's Supper is not mentioned in other passages concerning baptism, so it is not necessary here: one pertains to a person's *conversion* to Christ; the other, to his *continued devotion* to Him (see Coffman, *Commentary*, 198–199).

- **One Father.** God the Father is the head of the Godhead (1 Cor. 8:5–6, 11:3). He is "over all" regarding His sovereign authority; He is "through all" regarding His transcendence over all that has been created; and He is "in all" regarding His omnipresence in all that is alive—and especially in His church. From the Father comes the life, authority, and ability for all created entities to exist and function (recall 3:14–15). He is the source of all love, truth, justice, and salvation; He is the beginning and end of all Creation (Rev. 1:8).

Christ's Gifts to His Church (Eph. 4:7–16)

Christ's Victory over the World (4:7–10): Having laid out some essential teachings required of believers, Paul now turns the reader's attention to what believers have received from Christ. "But to each one of us" (4:7) determines the context of this thought: what Paul says here speaks to the individual believer, not the entire church. Christ has given each member of His church "grace" in the form of specific *gifts*. This is not what we might call "saving grace" (the blood-bought forgiveness of sin) but refers to gifts *of* grace—those providential helps provided solely for believers (Rom. 12:3–8). Paul mentions the purpose of these gifts later; for now, he simply wants Christians to appreciate how *blessed* they are "in Christ." Yet the distribution of what *kind* of gifts or the *measurement* (or allotment) of each gift is Christ's to determine: He knows what is needed, what is best for each believer, and how each part will contribute to the whole.[162]

"'When He ascended on high'" (4:8)—the quote is from Psalm 68:18, depicting a procession of God's people streaming to His holy mountain, victorious over their enemies. In like manner, Paul alludes to Christ's ascension into heaven with a (figurative) procession of souls redeemed by His blood, released from their condemnation by His atoning sacrifice. It may appear that these souls have been held captive by their captor (Satan); the

---

[162] This is similar in thought to what the Holy Spirit did for the early church in providing and distributing *miraculous* gifts to Christians through the laying on of the apostles' hands (1 Cor. 12:4–7, 11). Yet there is no good reason to assume that Paul is referring to miraculous gifts in the present passage in *Ephesians*; the context simply does not support this.

reality is that Satan has never had such power and has never literally held a single soul captive. The *real* captivity that has imprisoned human souls is the divine condemnation incurred because of sins and transgressions (recall 2:1). Satan's part as the "strong man" (see Mat. 12:29) is to have *deceived* all sinners in the first place, accusing them of their own guilt, and enslaving them to the fear of divine judgment (Heb. 2:14–15, Rev. 12:10–11). Death is the penalty for sin (Rom. 6:23), and so Christ had to die to free men from the wages of their sin. When He ascended to the right hand of God after overcoming the power of death (Acts 2:33), He secured the salvation of all those who sought redemption from their own (spiritual) death—and those who continue to seek this redemption.[163]

"[A]nd He gave gifts to men"—a different rendering than Psalm 68:18; in the psalm, it is *men* who give gifts to *God*. Yet in the big-picture analysis, it is always God who gives far *better* and more *numerous* gifts to men than we could ever give to Him.[164] Christ the Conqueror shares the plunder of His conquest with those who are allied with Him; these gifts are incomparably greater than anything we could have acquired on our own. The imagery Paul uses here alludes to Israel's exodus out of Egypt. In that case, God led His people out of the "iron furnace" (Deut. 4:20) and into freedom; in doing so, they plundered their captors (see Exod. 3:21–22 and 12:35–36). Similarly, we have a picture of Christ opening the prison of spiritual captivity and handing gifts (of His choice) to each released soul. Such gifts are to be employed in the growth and development of His church on earth, as Paul will soon reveal. It is unnecessary to think that Paul refers here only to miraculous (or spiritual) gifts. The use of "gifts" does not always mean the

---

163 Paul presents a *picture* in this passage, not a literal scenario. In other words, we cannot conclude that the souls of faithful men and women who died prior to Christ had been languishing in a spiritual prison until the time of His death. Instead, they enjoyed the comfort of those who have been forgiven, even though the actual *price* for their forgiveness was not paid until the cross. Thus, Paul (and the psalmist he cites) portrays a scene of victory symbolized by the sinner's release from prison rather than attempting to literalize what happened.

164 One might ask, "How can Paul *change Scripture* to accommodate his explanation?" The truth is that Paul changed nothing; instead, he gave a complete or more accurate *interpretation* of Scripture, given what has happened since David penned Psalm 68. Whatever Paul wrote by inspiration *is itself* Scripture, so that his interpretation of other scriptures supersedes our own separate interpretations. The same Holy Spirit who inspired David also inspired Paul, and He never contradicts Himself.

ability to do miracles.[165] In 1 Cor. 13, Paul speaks at length about the *greatest* gift of all, which is love—a non-miraculous yet amazing gift that every believer can exercise.

Paul then provides a parenthetical thought concerning Christ's ascension to glory (4:9–10). It is impossible for Christ to have ascended into glory unless He had first *descended* into the humiliation of this world: the sequence here is crucial; the one event precedes the other. Those who are redeemed must believe in both actions: first, that Christ is "Lord," meaning that He has come from heaven and is God; second, that He has risen from the lowest depths of the human experience—namely, death itself, even death on a cross (Rom. 10:6–9 and Phil. 2:8). Thus, Christ has gone to both extremes to redeem men from divine condemnation. He could not have led anyone to victory if He had not Himself gone through this full experience of "descending" and "ascending." Through this, Christ was able to "fill [or, supply; complete; satisfy]" the entirety of God's eternal purpose (4:10; recall 3:11–12). His ministry of reconciliation has fulfilled (or completed) whatever was needed on earth as well as in heaven.

Christ's Gifts to His Church (4:11–13): Having ascended into glory, Christ imparts gifts to each individual believer who seeks redemption in Him. Yet He also gives gifts to the entire *body* of believers—gifts designed to help *all* believers collectively (4:11–13). It is important to see that all the gifts mentioned here are in the form of *people*. Similarly, a congregation's greatest resource and most important asset is not its building, bank account, or programs; it is its *members*—people.

"Apostles" (4:11) has a dual meaning: it can refer to the apostolic *office* (to which Paul belongs) or only in a general sense (like what Paul said of Titus—2 Cor. 8:23). Paul can be referring to either or both cases in this passage since both apply; yet the *order* in which he mentions "apostles" leans heavily toward the *office* of an apostle, as one personally commissioned by Christ. A similar argument applies to "prophets": some prophesy with miraculous ability; others prophesy (so to speak) by declaring the truth that

---

165 Regarding the actual word itself: in 1 Cor. 12:4, for example, "spiritual gifts" is from *charisma*, "a divine endowment"; in Eph. 4:8, it is from *doma*, "a [generic] present or gift" (James Strong, *Strong's Talking Greek-Hebrew Dictionary*, electronic edition [database © WORDsearch Corp.], G1390).

has already been revealed. Again, it appears that Paul lists these functions in descending order, in which case he still refers to those endowed miraculous gifts. "Evangelists" [lit., proclaimers of good news] in Paul's day referred more to traveling missionaries and church founders rather than the more sedentary church ministers that we are familiar with today. Prophets typically speak of the future (what God wants revealed) while evangelists speak of the past (what He has already revealed). In Paul's day, such men could be speaking by divine inspiration or simply repeating what had already been disclosed *through* such inspiration. "Pastors" and "teachers" are two functions of the same person (or role). Pastors [lit., shepherds] do not refer to pulpit ministers or preachers but elders (or overseers) whose responsibility it is to shepherd the flock which had appointed them (1 Peter 5:1–3). Such men are also supposed to teach as *part* of their shepherding (1 Tim. 5:17, 1 Thess. 5:12–13). These last three descriptors (evangelists, pastors, and teachers) can refer to those with miraculous ability or those with no such ability.

All such men, as well as the roles that they fulfill, represent Christ's "gifts" to His church. Their *purpose* (or objective) is explained in 4:12–13: they are meant to "equip," "build up," and bring maturity to the body of Christ.

- "equipping [or, perfecting]" means to fill up with what is lacking; to furnish what is needed; and/or to restore what has diminished. God is the source of the equipping of the church (Heb. 13:20–21), yet He uses men and their positions of responsibility within the church to fulfill this objective. The expressed purpose of this "equipping" is to prepare the church to serve, not simply to acquire knowledge. Christians filled with biblical knowledge are a great asset to the church, but not if they fail to put that knowledge to work.
- To "build up" means to edify or add to the construction (of a particular structure). Obviously, Christian men are not building up the church *instead* of Christ but are serving the will of Christ *in* their efforts. Building up is the opposite of tearing down (cf. Rom. 14:20 and 2 Cor. 13:10, for example).
- "until we all attain to the unity of the faith" (4:13)—the "we" here means Christians everywhere, not just the Ephesians; "the faith" means that belief system which the gospel defines rather than a person's individual

faith. This "unity of the faith" and a "mature man" are ideal goals of each generation of believers and do not refer to a singular, universal, or historical achievement. While Christ is already perfect and complete, His physical church on earth is a work in progress and is always in the state of *being* perfected through the work of the Spirit, "the knowledge of the Son of God" that is procured through His gospel, and the various gifts that Christ showers upon His people. The expectation is that every believer will strive for spiritual maturity in his own walk with God, even as the church collectively strives for this same thing in each generation of believers. Yet Paul also means that this process of growth and maturity will never cease while the physical church remains.

- "to the measure of the stature ... of Christ"—i.e., the *standard* or *criterion* by which the church's growth and maturity are measured is Christ Himself. The church's progress is not measured against the preferences or perceptions of its own members, and certainly not by any worldly estimations. (This same principle applies to a particular congregation as well as any given member: Christ is the final standard by which all are measured.) In other words, the church's identity, teaching, work, and objectives must be consistent with the One who established this body of believers. "The church, as a corporate man, must match Christ's stature, just as a man's physical body must be comparable to his head. Christ's body, His fullness (1:23; 3:19), must match Christ, the fullness of God."[166] Another scholar says, "The important lesson taught here is that not only apostles, prophets, evangelists, and those who are called 'pastors and teachers,' but the entire church should be engaged in spiritual labor. 'The universal priesthood of believers' is stressed here."[167]

The Church's Expected Growth (4:14–16): "As a result" (4:14)—i.e., since Christ has blessed His church with such gifts and resources, He expects growth and maturity. "Children" here has a negative context, referring to those who are immature, untaught, and inexperienced and yet *should* be further along (cf. Heb. 5:12–13). Every Christian begins as a (spiritual) child but none of us are to make a career of remaining in this condition. Our attitude must always be child-like (humble, faithful, innocent, etc.); yet our spiritual minds, conduct, and service to one another must be continually

---

166 JFB, *Commentary* (electronic), on 4:13.
167 Hendriksen, *NTC*, 198.

maturing (1 Cor. 14:20). "[T]ossed here and there" alludes to a boat upon a rough sea, being completely at the mercy of the waves and unable to follow a straight course. This describes Christians who are untaught, unstable, and therefore vulnerable to all sorts of myths, fables, erroneous doctrines, and other useless teachings (2 Tim. 2:14, Titus 1:10–11, and 2 Peter 3:14–18).[168] Such people are in a constant state of spiritual confusion and mental turmoil; they may hold to "a form of godliness" but have denied its power; they may be "always learning" but are "never able to come to the knowledge of the truth" (2 Tim. 3:3, 5). Not only this, but there are those who are deliberately and maliciously infiltrating the church with corruptive teachings, hoping to gain attention and followers (1 Tim. 6:3–5, 2 Peter 2:1–3).

The church must not be characterized by such infantile minds. Instead, Christ wants it led by sober-minded men and women who know the gospel and are capable of accurately representing it in their lives *and* their teaching (recall 4:1). We are to be "speaking the truth in love" (4:15)—i.e., in a manner consistent with the *doctrine* and *attitude* of Christ Himself. "Truth" refers to what is said; "in love" describes the motive and manner in which truth is spoken. "[W]e are to grow up in all aspects into ... Christ"—the natural and stated objective of Christ's body is to grow *up* (or upward) in conformity to its head (Rom. 8:29).[169] This instruction must affect *every aspect and function* of what we do as the body of Christ; it is hardly to be limited to what is done during a church service. Christ is the Source of the (universal) church's stability, power, and growth; He will be the reason for its success. Drawing on a literal human body for the purpose of illustration, Christ has "fitted together" the body of believers and is the joining substance of every structural "bone" (so to speak) of the spiritual church (4:16). He is also the One who makes functional each individual bodily organ with His

---

168 "Trickery" is from *kubeia*, from which we get "cube," a reference to the throwing of dice (Strong, *Dictionary* [electronic], G2940). "Paul's effective characterization of error and of errorists is surely drawn from his own experience. He had been in vessels that were drifting helplessly in waves and wind; he had seen soldiers and sailors use loaded dice to fleece some innocent greenhorn. They had their expert system which was all fair and honest to the inexperienced eye but deadly in its cunning and trickiness" (Lenski, *Interpretation*, 541).

169 Lenski disagrees with the translation, "into Him who is the head, {even} Christ," because we who are the body of Christ *never* grow "into" the head, or become anything different than the body (*Interpretation*, 544). This observation is accurate. Yet, despite the translators' choice of words, Christ alone is the head of His body, and that our endeavor is to become *like* Him in every aspect, while never duplicating or replacing Him.

body, causing all these parts to work together as a singular, living organism. In other words, there are no unwanted, useless, or expendable "parts" within Christ's church; every single member is valuable and designed to contribute to the whole body. "In love" dictates the *reason* or *ultimate motive* behind all that Christ does for His church *and* all that the church does for Him. Godly love [Greek, *agape*] always serves the best interest of the one to whom it is demonstrated (Col. 3:14).

Section Four: The Christian's Walk (4:17—6:9)

Putting on the "New Self" (Eph. 4:17–24)

The Spiritual Darkness of the Unconverted (4:17–19): Paul now resumes the thought he began in the opening of this chapter. "Gentiles" often means *the unconverted*, regardless of race, but specifically Paul refers to those pagan-minded, idolatrous people (who are not Jews) that put confidence in useless things rather than in God (4:17–19; see Rom. 1:21–32). He admonishes the Ephesians—many of whom came out of the very lifestyle and culture described here—to no longer continue in that walk. The "futile" life of an unbeliever is incompatible with the believer's life with the Spirit (2 Cor. 6:14–16, Gal. 5:16–17, 25).

While Paul has a certain lifestyle in mind as he writes these words, it would be wrong for us to limit his description to the ancient world. People today may not be bowing down to idols, making meat sacrifices to imaginary gods, participating in cultic temple prostitution, etc., but godless, unspiritual, and greed-driven lifestyles are common to our modern culture. Likewise, many people today are indoctrinated with empty philosophies (Col. 2:8), led astray by wicked deceptions of every kind, and spiritually bankrupt. Regardless, Paul describes people who are:

- **futile in their mind.** This refers to a kind of thinking or mentality that simply offers no genuine spiritual advantage to the one who embraces it. Paul may have in mind the Greek philosophies of Epicureanism, Stoicism, or of Persian Zoroastrianism, or any of the idolatries commonly practiced in his day. Today, we might think of evolutionism, existentialism, humanism, agnosticism, or atheism. All such beliefs are pointless, hopeless, and spiritually vacant—the godless products of human imagination. Modern philosophies and religions that deny the irrepressible truth of God's existence imitate ancient degenerate thinking (Rom. 1:18–22).

- **darkened in their understanding.** "Darkened" here contrasts with (spiritual) illumination. Many intelligent, well-educated people today believe themselves to be enlightened through secular knowledge and philosophic pursuits, yet the opposite may be true. Jesus came to enlighten people *with* truth, but He also acknowledged that not everyone is genuinely interested in this (John 3:18–21). Satan blinds the hearts of the unbelieving (2 Cor. 4:3–4); the more a person denies the truth and resists God's spiritual influence, the darker his mind becomes until he is engulfed *in* darkness (2 Thess. 2:10–12). "It is a serious punishment to have to suffer the consequences of one's own evil choices, without the benefit of corrective guidance."[170] Another scholar says, "Not only is it true that people of this kind dwell in the darkness, but the darkness dwells in them."[171]

- **excluded from the life of God.** This ("the life of God") is a unique phrase in Scripture, likely referring to fellowship *with* God as well as living in the presence *of* God. Being excluded from this life makes us think of Adam and Eve being banished from the Garden, driven from the intimate and uncorrupted fellowship they had enjoyed with God in that Paradise. The ancient pagans and idolaters, as well as modern philosophers and atheists who cling to hopeless beliefs, were likewise excluded from this fellowship. While it is God who does the excluding, their *resistance to the truth* is the cause of it.

- **filled with ignorance.** While religious and superstitious ignorance filled the ancient world, the gospel has dispelled this darkness with light and truth. God once tolerated this ignorance (to a degree) until further revelation came; but now that divine revelation has come in the form of His incarnate Son, men have no excuse for this (John 15:22, Acts 17:30–31). Paul does not describe an insurmountable condition, but one *chosen* either through deliberate rejection of the truth or by failing to discern truth from error.

- **hardened in their heart.** "Hardness" (as used in Scripture to define the human heart) refers to a conscience insensitive to God's message, callous to His warnings, and untouched by His kindness. The conscience that repeatedly rejects God's truth becomes completely unresponsive to it (as depicted in 1 Tim. 4:1–3). While God may *further* one's already-

---

170 JFB, *Commentary* (electronic), on 4:19.
171 Hendriksen, *NTC*, 210.

hardened heart by continuing to give him opportunity to repent (that He knows will be forfeited), as in the celebrated case of Pharaoh (Rom. 9:17–18), responsibility for such hardness lies with the one who rejects God, not with God who has been rejected. Hardness (like apostasy) is not limited to a single incident but is a condition that happens over time.

- **practicers of sensuality and impurity.** "Sensuality" refers to unbridled lust (or sexual passion), wantonness, or shamelessness. It describes illicit indulgence in carnal pleasures, as seen today in pornography, homosexuality, promiscuity, prostitution, sadomasochism, and any other aberrant sexual practices. "Impurity" refers to any morally-unclean behavior—thus, anything which violates the natural order of Creation and procreation as established by God from the beginning.
- **greedy.** Paul has not suddenly shifted his thought to money (although the principles stated here do apply to this). "Greediness" (or covetousness) is a corruptive desire of the human heart toward all *kinds* of things, including money (Exod. 20:17, Luke 12:15). Greed and idolatry go together; greed is a basic manifestation *of* idolatry (Eph. 5:5, Col. 3:5). Those who are unsatisfied with God and what He offers will greedily desire (or covet) that which He has forbidden.

The Enlightenment of Believers (4:20–24): "But you did not learn Christ in this way" (4:20). Paul's gospel does not teach or cater to such inferior and morally deficient means of instruction. Whatever comes from God is good, wholesome, and full of light (James 1:17); it is uncontaminated from illicit desires or human philosophies. The way God calls Christians (recall 4:1) does not involve the base elements of this world but transcends such hopeless thinking. To "learn [or, know] Christ" does not mean merely to know *about* Him but to have fellowship *with* Him because of a spiritual re-creation in God (recall 2:10; see 2 Cor. 5:17). This begins with *hearing* (of) Him (Rom. 10:17); being *taught* about Him (John 20:31); and then [implied] *putting faith* in Him (4:21). Jesus is the embodiment *of* truth, as He Himself has said (John 14:6); but Paul also means that His message (or gospel) is "the truth" (recall 1:13; see Col. 1:5). The truth revealed in Christ will *never* lead a person to conduct himself in an ungodly and impure manner. On the contrary, believers are to be holy and pure in all their behavior (1 Peter 1:13–16, 1 John 3:3).

Only when one fully surrenders his "former manner of life" or "old self" can he put on the "new self" (4:22–24). Corruption always leads to destruction: whatever man corrupts, God eventually destroys. Thus, the "old self" is effectively destroyed in one's symbolic death, burial, and resurrection to newness of life, as depicted by his baptism (Rom. 6:3–7). Instead of marrying the "old" with the "new," one "self" must be removed for the other to take its place. This means there is no compatibility between the two lives; God only supports the "new self" and no other. Obviously, this is explained in an idealistic sense, since believers put on the "new man" every day, just as they take up their cross every day (Luke 9:23). While this "[putting] on the new self" has an event-oriented, historical *beginning* (in baptism), it is thereafter an ongoing process in which one is continuously improving from day to day (2 Cor. 4:16).[172] This "new self" has been created *by* God and is consistent with His nature. Yet it is not God who puts it on each individual believer; that is the responsibility of the believer himself. God provides, but He does not force; He supplies, but He does not impose. "Man is fitted for union with God only in so far as he follows the teachings of Jesus."[173]

Not That, But This
(Eph. 4:25—5:21)

In this section, Paul begins a lengthy series of contrasting "walks" to provide practical application of what he has just said. This creates a "not that, but this"-kind of teaching, which is informative on both sides of the equation and leaves little to speculation. In each case, "old self" behavior must be laid aside for "new self" behavior to be implemented. It is quickly apparent, too, that even though God gives each believer a "new self," this new creation interweaves with the entire body of Christ. In other words, one's individual behavior and the corporate behavior must agree; each member as well as the entire body must agree with the head (Christ).

---

172 "It is quite true that the old man still clings to us after the decisive break [i.e., baptism—MY WORD] and thus must be put away again and again. That is why Paul adds the iterative present infinitive, 'but that you continue to be renewed,' etc. Paul's view is: one definite, decisive break and then a continuous renewal" (Lenski, *Interpretation*, 563–564).

173 Lipscomb, *Commentary*, 87.

What to put away: falsehood (4:25). This is a general term that refers to any spoken lie, dishonesty, deception, or fakery.[174] God has *always* condemned falsehood in every covenant He has made with men (Exod. 20:16, Prov. 6:16–19, Col. 3:9–10, etc.). Such conduct has no place in the body of Christ or in the "new self."

What to practice instead: truth. God *is* truth, and there is no lie or "shifting shadow" within Him (Titus 1:2, James 1:17); "no lie is of the truth" (1 John 2:21). Likewise, those who belong to Him must also be truthful and straightforward in all their actions. If we are spiritually *bound* to one another in Christ, we are to honor this fellowship with our words. The honesty and integrity we express to one another must reflect (and agree with) the sincerity by which we conduct ourselves before God Himself.

What to put away: prolonged, self-serving anger (4:26–27). Likely, Paul quotes from Psalm 4:4; regardless, his own inspired words have become our Scripture. Anger is a God-given emotion and thus has its place in the Christian life. Yet personal anger that arises from one's indignation over someone having affronted *oneself* (rather than righteous anger over that which offends *God*) is a different matter. Such anger is not from God but can easily become a tool of Satan, especially when it stews and smolders within a person's heart. Sustained anger can serve as a catalyst for all sorts of wicked actions; this is the "opportunity" an angry person gives to Satan.

What to practice instead: resolution and reconciliation [implied]. Jesus taught that reconciliation with our "brother" is a priority to bringing an offering to God (Mat. 5:23–24). If something happens between brethren that disrupts the concord and fellowship between them, this needs rectification—and without delay. Forbearance, forgiveness, and harmony are what characterizes Christ's church; these virtues begin with each member doing his part in pursuit of them.

---

174 "Falsehood is translated from the Greek word *pseudos*. We anglicize that word as a prefix to many English words suggesting 'pretended reality.' Falsehood is fiction. It claims something which is not so. The key to the sinfulness of one involved in falsehood is misrepresentation and deception" (Caldwell, *Ephesians*, 206).

What to put away: stealing (4:28). Thievery is a lowly and yet all-too-common crime among ungodly people. Taking what does not belong to you—whether it be money, a personal possession, an animal, an inheritance, or even a spouse—is always wicked in God's sight (Exod. 20:15, Rom. 13:9). Those who practice such things will not inherit the kingdom of God (1 Cor. 6:9–10).

What to practice instead: legitimate and gainful employment. Since stealing and idleness often go together, Paul admonishes those who once made their living by thievery to find a job and earn money through legitimate and honest labor. Instead of *taking* things from others, Christians are to be generous *givers*, and especially to the brotherhood (Rom. 12:13, 2 Cor. 8:1–5). This also means that Christians are not to be lazy, undisciplined, or irresponsible and thus become a liability to the brethren; "If anyone is not willing to work, then he is not to eat, either" (see 2 Thess. 3:6–12). God is honored by Christians' productive activity and industriousness; this is the kind of lifestyle we are to pursue.

What to put away: unwholesome words (4:29). "Unwholesome" means rotten, morally corrupt, or worthless. This covers a wide spectrum of speech and conversation: unfair characterizations, unloving criticism, spite-filled comments, insinuating implications, hateful retorts, or any mean or unchristian words.

What to practice instead: gracious words of edification. "Edification" is the process of building up, never tearing down. Our words must be purposely chosen and designed to build up one another through sincere encouragement, never empty flattery or hollow praise. "[A]ccording to the need of the moment" means that we should be perceptive *to* such needs and frame our words to accommodate them. Just as God has showered us with saving grace, so we are to reflect this same sort of kindness toward one another (Col. 4:6). The adage "If you can't say something nice, then don't say anything at all" seems to apply here as well.

What to put away: grieving the Holy Spirit (4:30). *All* behaviors that must be put away bring grief to God's Spirit, so this instruction has broad application. More specifically, when the inspired word of God clearly instructs one thing and we do quite another, this brings grief to the Holy

Spirit since He is the Author of that word. Whenever a believer refuses to "walk by the Spirit," this is a source of sadness and disappointment to God—the exact opposite of what we ought to produce in Him. Rebellion (or disobedience) against God is always sinful, regardless of the nature of that rebellion (1 Sam. 15:23).[175]

What to practice instead: obedience to God's word [implied]. God takes great delight in the one who is "humble and contrite of spirit, and who trembles at my word" (Isa. 66:2b). Obedience to His word also honors the One who has revealed and preserved that word for this very purpose: God's Holy Spirit. It is through our initial obedience to God that we were "sealed for the day of redemption" (see 2 Cor. 1:21–22; recall 1:13–14); we are expected to continue in that same walk thereafter (Gal. 5:16, 25).

What to put away: all bitterness, wrath, anger, clamor, slander, and malice (4:31). These are the characteristics of a heart conditioned and hardened by the world; they are "deeds of the flesh," not "fruit of the Spirit" (Gal. 5:19–23). "Bitterness" refers to the sustained, poisonous hatred of one's heart. "Wrath" and "anger" reveal the self-serving, vengeful spirit of one who allows his emotions to dictate his behavior. "Clamor" can refer to any kind of noise or tumult, indicating one's chaotic or out-of-control disposition or lifestyle. "Clamor is the loud self-assertion of an angry man, who attempts to make everyone hear his grievance."[176] "Slander" [lit., blasphemy] means to speak evil (or rail) against someone, especially God. "Malice" is the intention to do harm to someone; more generally, it is any sort of wickedness or evil behavior that is directed toward another.

What to practice instead: kindness, tender-heartedness, and forgiveness (4:32). Such spiritual virtues are the exact opposite of what Paul has just described. "Kindness" is a general term denoting all sorts of expressions of goodness, gentleness, or integrity. Those led by God's Spirit extend kindness and gentleness in dealing with others, and especially those in need of instruction (Col. 3:12–13, 2 Tim. 2:25, James 3:13, and 1 Peter 3:15). "Tender-hearted" indicates compassion, mercy,

---

175 For further study on this subject, I recommend my book, *The Holy Spirit of God: A Biblical Perspective*; go to www.spiritbuilding.com/chad.

176 Lipscomb, *Commentary*, 95.

and sympathy (or empathy). "Forgiveness" is the act of absolving a debt incurred by another person with a view toward God's forgiveness of our own debts (Mat. 6:14–15). "God had to give up his only Son to forgive us ... we have to give up nothing but our selfish natures to forgive our brother."[177]

"Therefore" (5:1)—i.e., since these things are true: God has made Christ the head of His church; He has given all sorts of gifts and resources to this church; those who are in the church are renewed by the Spirit of God and no longer walk according to the world; and the characteristics of this "new self" are (to be) actively demonstrated in everyday life. To "be imitators of God" does not mean "become a divine being," but "learn to internalize the nature of your Father." As adopted sons, Christians are to adopt the virtues of the One who adopted them and no longer practice the behavior of natural, human conditioning. This requires that they live in a manner defined by and consistent with God's divine love, since God *is* love (5:2; see 1 Cor. 13:4–7, 1 John 4:7–8). Christ's death on the cross on our behalf is the clearest expression of this love.

"Offering" and "sacrifice" (5:2) are virtually identical, yet (drawing on the Levitical sacrificial system) "offering" generally refers to a gift presented to God, and "sacrifice" refers to a slain animal that is put upon the altar—i.e., a blood-sacrifice. "Fragrant aroma" alludes to the "soothing aroma" of pleasing sacrifices offered to God under the Law (Lev. 1:9, 4:31, etc.). Christians do not offer blood sacrifices to God since Christ has fulfilled "once for all" the blood sacrifice required of God (Heb. 10:10–14). We do, however, offer ourselves as a "living and holy sacrifice" in the form of active servitude in whatever measure God requires of us (Rom. 12:1–2). This is the sense of Paul's words here: we are not "begotten" sons like Christ was, but we can learn to imitate God's nature; we are not able to duplicate the offering and sacrifice of Christ, but we can pattern our own lives in honor of what He did. Having said this, Paul returns to his "not that, but this" formula:

What to put away: immorality, impurity, and greed (5:3). These are very general terms with broad application. They describe, however, a specific kind of person—one who is carnal-minded, self-serving, and

---

177 JFB, *Commentary* (electronic), on 4:32.

under the influence of Satan rather than the Holy Spirit. "Immorality" comes from *porneia*, from which we get "pornography"; it refers to all kinds of sexual sin (fornication, adultery, incest, prostitution, etc.). A "sexual sin" is any deviation from the natural order of Creation—i.e., the sexual behavior exclusively between a husband and his wife. "Impurity" refers to any physical or moral uncleanness (such as illicit fantasies, inappropriate physical contact, participation in any ungodly behavior, crudity, etc.; see 1 Thess. 4:3–7). "Greed" has many forms, and we are warned to avoid all of them (Luke 12:15). In general, greed (or covetousness) is one's self-serving, carnal appetite for that which he does not already have, intended for his own personal gain.

What to practice instead: sexual propriety, moral cleanness, and contentment (in God) [implied]. Throughout his epistles, Paul deals quite a bit with sexual sins, since these typify the carnal, sensual, and self-gratifying nature of worldly-minded people. The opposite of this behavior, however, is chaste, pure, legitimate, and self-controlled behavior. This befits one who has discipline of character, temperance, and structure; it necessarily implies a mastery over one's thoughts, conduct, emotions, and desires (2 Peter 1:6). One who finds his contentment in God (rather than in this world) will funnel his desires and energies toward heavenly pursuits rather than seek sensual and temporary gratification in this life.

What to put away: filthiness, silly talk, and coarse jesting (5:4). Simply put, Paul refers to the gutter language of the world, which includes profanity, empty or useless talk, dirty jokes, and vulgar words. Today, we would characterize this as "talking garbage," "trash-talking," or being a "potty-mouth." Those who wish to fit in with the world will also learn to speak its language; "for even the way you talk gives you away" (Mat. 26:73). The world endorses those who speak *like* the world (1 John 4:5), but God will not extend His holy fellowship to such people.
What to practice instead: the giving of thanks. Expressing gratitude forces a person to focus upon the more serious matters of life, and raises one's view far above the empty, crude, and irreverent talk of ungrateful men (Col. 4:2). While ingratitude and irreverence always go together, so do sincere gratitude and holy reverence. "Giving of thanks brings about

the real joy of the spirit that the worldly try to achieve with their style of humor and communication."[178]

What to put away: immorality, impurity, and covetousness (or greed) (5:5–7). These thoughts re-state what has just been said (5:3). Any illicit or excessive devotion given to anything or anyone that robs God of His rightful pre-eminence in a person's heart is idolatry. It is coveting—that dark, satanic, greedy desire of the heart—that *prompts* such illicit devotion in the first place. Those who act upon these desires and give their devotion to something other than God have no inheritance with Him: God will not welcome and reward idolaters. "Let no one deceive you"—i.e., do not be conned, convinced, or deceived into thinking otherwise. A common strategy of worldly people is to re-package their wicked behavior as something harmless, beneficial, or profitable. Such are the "empty words" spoken by people destined to face God's wrath for their failure to honor Him *as* God (John 3:36, Rom. 2:8, Col. 3:6, etc.).

What to practice instead: walking as children of light (in goodness, righteousness, and truth) and learning what is pleasing to the Lord (5:8–10). The believer's spiritual birth is *because* the "Light of the world" has come into his heart, leading to his born-again fellowship with God (John 1:9–13). He is no longer (merely) a child of the flesh but is (much more) a child of God. His objective, then, is to live in a manner consistent with his calling and spiritual birth. Collectively, Christians are not just "in" the light, but they are "Light in the Lord" (see Mat. 5:14). "Goodness," "righteousness," and "truth" are mutually dependent: by practicing one, a person must uphold the others. Goodness defines God's motive ("This is why I should act"); righteousness defines His actual practice ("This is the right action"); and truth defines His criterion for acting ("This is the moral absolute upon which right action is based"). "[T]rying to learn what is pleasing to the Lord" indicates that the believer is not miraculously or immediately endowed with such knowledge or understanding. Instead, he must *learn* this information through what God has revealed, which requires diligent study of His word (2 Tim. 2:15).

---

[178] JFB, *Commentary* (electronic), on 5:4.

What to put away: unfruitful deeds of darkness (5:11a). This general phrase can include *anything* that stands opposed to the Light (see Gal. 5:19–21). Such actions are "unfruitful" because they produce nothing but spiritual death to the one who practices them (Rom. 6:23). The believer is to "lay aside the deeds of darkness and put on the armor of light" (Rom. 13:12–14). Instead of partaking in the sinful deeds of sinful men, he is to put on Christ and make *no provision* (or give no place) for wicked desires to take root in his heart.

What to practice instead: exposing the deeds of darkness with the Light (5:11b–13). "The light" serves two purposes: first, to expose error and wickedness; second, to illuminate with truth and righteousness. No one can embrace the truth of God until he first acknowledges the error and wickedness which has engulfed his heart; thus, "If we say that we have no sin, we are deceiving ourselves and the truth is not in us" (1 John 1:8). Likewise, when dealing with a sinful world, one cannot simply preach the truth, but in doing so he must also expose the error. It is this double-edged sword that makes the gospel message so repulsive to the unrepentant heart: not only does it expose the sinner's lies and criminal activity, but it also introduces the *right* way to live that compels him to give up those lies. "[E]verything that becomes visible is light"— or, "Whatever the light exposes for what it really is can no longer remain shrouded in (the) darkness." For example, when the gospel exposes the *truth* of one's sinful condition, his condition is no longer justifiable or defensible; what he *thought* was "true" has been exposed as a lie, and the *reality* of his situation now is revealed. (He can still deny this truth, but no one ever made the truth disappear by denying it.)

What to put away: spiritual inactivity and/or insensitivity to the word (5:14). The "dead" must refer to those who remain outside of God's fellowship (recall 2:1); those who "sleep" refers to those who have been born again but then lulled into a state of inactivity or indifference (see Rom. 13:11–12, 1 Thess. 5:6, and Rev. 3:2–3). In either case, it is Christ who can bring a person out of his spiritual death or rouse him to action—*if* a person will allow Him to enlighten his heart.

What to practice instead: active, demonstrated obedience to Christ [implied]. One who is enlightened has a responsibility to act upon that new information; he cannot remain unchanged. Discipleship is never a static, inactive state, but is characterized by work and servitude (Rom. 12:9–18, for example).[179]

What to put away: walking as unwise men, wasting time, and being foolish (5:15–17). Such admonition makes sense: conversion to Christ, knowledge of the truth, and the enlightenment of the heart *never* leads to foolish or unprofitable conduct. Wisdom, time, and knowledge are precious and priceless commodities; we cannot afford to squander or exchange them for lesser things. Foolish people—this is God's definition, not ours—are those who either refuse to believe in God (despite all the evidence provided; Rom. 1:21–22) or who claim to be "of God" yet choose to remain ignorant of His will.

What to practice instead: walking as wise men, being good stewards of our time, and understanding what the will of the Lord is. Not only are we to strive to please God, but we must strive to act becomingly, circumspectly (or carefully), and knowledgeably before others (Col. 4:5–6, Titus 2:7–8, 1 Peter 3:15). In other words, appropriate *outward behavior* demonstrates *inward enlightenment*. "The one who says, 'I have come to know Him,' and does not keep His commandments, is a liar, and the truth is not in him; but whoever keeps His word, in him the love of God has truly been perfected" (1 John 2:4–5).

What to put away: drunkenness and dissipation (i.e., wasteful indulgence; harmful excessiveness) (5:18). Drunkenness depicts worldly excess and self-gratification, which results in unchristian behavior and an out-of-control state of being. "Drunkenness" (or dissipation) is hardly limited to drinking alcohol but can apply to any overindulgence or lifestyle of excess that exhibits a lack of discipline or self-control (i.e., gluttony, smoking, drug use, gambling, sexually arousing entertainment, profanity, etc.).

What to practice instead: being filled with the Spirit, speaking psalms and singing hymns to one another, giving thanks to God, and being subject to one another (5:19). Paul is not making a direct connection here between the outward effects of alcohol and the Spirit (as though, "Be drunk with the Spirit, not wine"). Rather, he focuses

---

[179] Hendriksen suggests that this hymn-like passage may be an adaptation of Isa. 60:1, especially since Paul wrote these words with hymns in mind (*NTC*, 235).

on what "fills" the Christian versus what fills the pleasure-seeking unconverted person. The believer is to be filled with the Spirit, not alcohol; he is to express himself in the form of speaking psalms and songs (for mutual edification) and hymns (in praise of God), not undisciplined and reckless behavior. Being "filled with the Spirit" does not refer to a miraculous experience or the ability to perform miracles. Instead, Paul implies that there ought to be an outward manifestation of the Spirit's presence in the believer's heart—and this way will be far different than the "spirit" of an ungodly person.

Instructions for Singing and Subjection (5:19–21): In classical Greek, "making melody" [*psallo*] meant "to twang or pluck," as one would do on a stringed instrument (5:19). Many people have used this definition to validate the use of musical instruments in collective worship to God. Such reasoning goes beyond merely stretching Paul's point, but completely misinterprets it.[180] It is context which defines *how* a word is used, whether literally or figuratively. We cannot impose a literal interpretation upon a figurative use or application of a word. On that point, consider the following:

- Paul is discussing how Christians can share *themselves* with one another (in spiritual fellowship), not how they can play an instrument for one another.
- If a person demands that Paul means "play musical instruments" here, then every Christian that did *not* play an instrument would be in violation of this passage. This would forbid all *a capella* (or vocal-only) singing.[181] Furthermore, all Christians would have to play their musical instruments simultaneously to fulfill this instruction.
- As it is, Paul never instructed the church to play instruments but to sing *words* ("speaking") that come from *the heart* (not "plucking" with the hands). Thus, he qualifies or modifies the *kind* of music practiced among God's people: it is vocal music, for the purpose of collective worship and praise.
- An instrument cannot replace what the human heart alone can do. An

---

180 "Arguments from the ancient meaning of *psallo* are, as F. F. Bruce declared, 'irrelevant to the question of instrumental music, one way or the other'" (Coffman, *Commentary*, 221).

181 *A capella* literally means "in the chapel style," with reference to the centuries of religious hymn-singing (dating from pre-Medieval Era) that was entirely vocalized without musical accompaniment.

- instrument cannot "give thanks" or "be subject" to another person. Paul speaks of what believers *personally* do for one another, not something they do through a separate medium.
- Speaking *spiritual* psalms and hymns are, in this context, expressions of a heart that is filled with God's Spirit.[182] This is something any genuine believer can do; it is not limited to those who know how to play an instrument.
- Teaching and admonishing (Col. 3:16) are things that Christians do personally *with* one another as well as *for* one another. An instrument can neither teach nor admonish.
- To read "with musical instruments" into this passage puts something into the text that simply is not there. Christians are never told simply to "make music" but to "speak" and "sing" *in a most personal manner*.
- Singing together is a fellowship (or communal) experience: it is not something you watch or listen to but something in which believers (jointly) participate. Singing is a unique expression of collective worship: at no other time do Christians come together *with their own voices* in a singular activity of praise to God *and* edification to one another.
- Just because we *can* do something does not mean we *ought* to do it. Likewise, just because someone "feels" a certain practice does not violate what Paul has instructed Christians everywhere does not automatically make it permissible. Human feelings and preferences are illegitimate standards for determining practices for the entire brotherhood. It is Christ's church we belong to, not our own; He is its head, not us.
- Vocal singing is something Christians are instructed to do; playing instruments *while* singing (or *instead* of singing) are man-made additions to or re-definitions of this instruction. This addition does not just "supplement" or "expedite" the instruction but changes either the *action* or the *purpose* for it entirely. The reason for this inclusion boils down to one thing: people like to *hear* and/or *play* musical instruments. This practice becomes a seemingly justifiable form of entertainment rather than an opportunity to fulfill our moral obligations to one another.

---

[182] "God is concerned with the inner man. He concentrates on our hearts and not on the aesthetic sound. He wishes melody made with the heart, not the harp. He does not want hypocritical or pretentious worship. Neither does he want lip-service which has no spiritual quality" (Caldwell, *Ephesians*, 258).

- Those who justify musical instruments in collective worship as a "scriptural expedient" fail to understand the concept *of* expediency in Scripture (1 Cor. 6:12, 10:23, 31–33).[183] A practice is expedient—i.e., facilitates the carrying out of an authorized command without changing it—only if it is *lawful, profitable* (in essence, advancing the cause of Christ), and *edifying*. Instrumental music, by contrast, is not commanded: it cannot be a "command" and optional all at once. It is not "profitable," since it is a human innovation and not something Christ requires of His church. Many people attempt to circumvent this by re-defining *profitable* as *pleasurable* ("I like the piano; it helps me to worship God"). Yet nothing that imposes upon God's directive can be profitable to believers; and we dare not define worship to God by personal pleasures. Finally, it is not "edifying" since musical instruments continue to be a source of controversy, division, and subjective interpretation within the brotherhood. (Read Rom. 14:19–20 and replace "food" with "instrumental music" and "eats" with "worships with instruments," for example.) The congregation that employs musical instruments *imposes its own form of worship* upon every member in that congregation—even those whose consciences are violated by participating in that kind of "worship." This is not expediency; it is forced indoctrination.

Our purpose here is to understand *what Paul said* (and did *not* say) in this passage (5:19) rather than delve into the subject of "instrumental music." Songs of praise include many thanksgivings (5:20): expressed gratitude *for* God and worship *of* God go together; it is impossible to do the one without necessarily involving the other. "[A]nd be subject to one another" (5:21)—i.e., every Christian ought to regard every other Christian as more important than himself (Rom. 15:2, Phil. 2:3–4). "Subject" [Greek, *hupotasso*] here means to voluntarily put oneself under the control of another; to yield to (the authority, position, or advice) of another. This warns against any abuse of power or position within the brotherhood. This also introduces a brief coverage of earthly relationships among spiritual believers (5:22—6:9).

---

183 For further study on this subject, I strongly recommend my book, *The New Testament Pattern: God's Plan for Christians and Their Churches*; go to www.spiritbuilding.com/chad.

The Marriage Relationship
(Eph. 5:22–33)

So far, Paul has been making general statements that apply to the entire brotherhood equally. Yet Christians have specific earthly relationships—within the family as well as society—and need to know how to function *as* Christians in those relationships. What follows is admittedly brief, especially considering the commonness of these relationships and the scope of their effect over the course of one's life. Nonetheless, its brevity allows this instruction to transcend all eras and cultures since these relationships are present in every society.[184] Furthermore, Paul's instruction for husbands and wives elevates the marriage relationship to a more mature perspective than was commonly practiced in his day (and in most of human history).

Instructions to Christian Wives (5:22–24): "Wives, {be subject} to your own husbands, as to the Lord" (5:22). The phrase "be subject" is not in the Greek text but is necessarily implied because of the preceding verse and what follows; otherwise, it makes no sense at all. "Subject" [Greek, *hupotasso*] is a military term, meaning "to rank under (another)." It has nothing to do with the character or value of the person who subjects himself (or herself) but has specific reference to one's standing, rank, or position *relative to another's*. Thus, it is a comparative term ("This is *different* than that"), not an evaluative one ("This is *better* than that"). Until a woman becomes her husband's wife, she is to submit to every man alike. Once she becomes her husband's wife, however, she accepts a different *kind* of submission. She is still in subjection *generally* to all men, given the natural order of Creation (1 Cor. 11:3),[185] but now she is in subjection *specifically* to her husband ("to your own husbands," not to all husbands equally).[186] A Christian wife is to voluntarily put herself

---

184 Some say, "Slavery has been eradicated in America, and so the 'master-slave' part of Paul's instruction is no longer relevant to us." Perhaps some forms of slavery have been eradicated (for now), but the principle of a master and (virtual) slave is perpetuated even in our modern labor system. As long as there are Christian employers and Christian employees, Paul's words will still serve as a guiding instruction for those people.

185 I recommend my *1 Corinthians Commentary* (Spiritbuilding Publishers) for a much more detailed explanation of 1 Cor. 11:3; go to www.spiritbuilding.com/chad.

186 "The wife is told to 'submit' in the husband-wife relationship, whereas children are taught to 'obey,' for there is greater equality between spouses than between parents and children" (JFB, *Commentary* [electronic], on 5:22).

under the control of her husband for the following reasons:

- ❏ This is how God instituted the marriage relationship from the beginning.
- ❏ There is a need for law and order within the marriage (and family), and God has made the husband the "head" authority in that relationship.
- ❏ This is the Holy Spirit-inspired instruction to Christian wives.
- ❏ God has never put women in authority over men in any of His revelations to the church (1 Cor. 11:8–9, 1 Tim. 2:13).
- ❏ This relationship is patterned after Christ and His church, and therefore must be honored by those *in* His church.

The wife's subjection to her husband does not make her morally inferior to him in any respect; this is simply a matter of *authority* and *propriety*. Christ is not morally inferior to His Father, yet He subjects Himself to the Father's authority even now (compare Mat. 28:18 and 1 Cor. 15:27–28). The church—in her glorified, bride-like state—is not morally inferior to Christ, yet she subjects herself to His authority and oversight. No Christian is morally inferior to any other Christian, yet we are told to subject ourselves to one another (recall 5:21). The point is: subjection is not a negative thing, but is a factual, historical, and necessary thing.[187]

Our modern hyper-sensitive, politically correct agenda to make women equal to men in *every respect* opposes this godly instruction. Yet Christianity has leveled the playing field (so to speak) between men and women as much as is possible without violating the natural order of Creation. In Christ, men and women are equals; in Christ, husbands and wives are equals as children of God (Gal. 3:28–29). But "in Christ" defines a spiritual relationship, not an earthly one; our spiritual relationship with Christ does not automatically make our earthly relationships invalid. On earth, as far as God is concerned, men still have more authority than women, husbands are still the heads of their wives, parents are still honored above their children, and masters

---

[187] "This submission of the wife, when rightly understood and practiced, accords with her inner nature, is in harmony with her relations to God and others, and is productive of the fullest development of her character, her highest happiness and good" (Lipscomb, *Commentary*, 111). Caldwell says: "She [the wife], in fact, regards her obedience to him [in the act of submission] as an act of obedience to Christ and as a part of her submission to the Lord" (*Ephesians*, 267; bracketed words are mine). In other words, submission to one's husband is not a separate issue from one's submission to the Lord, but the two actions are seen as two sides of the same coin.

still have authority over slaves. Social movements or cultural influences cannot override God's prescription for proper earthly relationships. We are Christians *before* and *regardless* of whether we are married, citizens of a given society, or part of a given culture.

"For the husband is the head of the wife" (5:23–24). The wife demonstrates her obedience to Christ through her submission to her husband; likewise, she is disobedient to Christ when she refuses to subject herself to her husband. Thus, the genuineness of one relationship is dependent upon the genuineness of the other. "Head" implies a positive oversight or management of those who have subjected themselves *to* it. Christ is the Savior of His spiritual bride; similarly, the Christian husband is to shepherd, protect, nurture, and lead his wife heavenward—especially through his own godly example. His Christian wife is a "fellow heir" of the promises (1 Peter 3:7), and not a lesser recipient than himself—and certainly not morally inferior to him. When Paul says, "in everything," he means *in everything*. The only [implied] exception to this would be if a husband forced his wife to violate God's word and/or her own conscience.[188] He cannot expect her to "be subject" to him while forcing her to sin against God; this is twisted logic. But in any other case, he has the final say. This does not mean his wife has *no* say and that she cannot inspire him to reason better than he might have on his own. It simply means that he is the head, and she is not. Both parties must respect—and be responsible toward—their respective roles within the marriage.

Instructions to Christian Husbands (5:25–30): "Husbands, love your wives" (5:25–27). The marriage relationship is based upon love and respect.[189] Both love *and* respect are to be given unconditionally by the husband and wife, respectively. He does not love her "if" or "when" or "because"; he loves her *always* and *anyway*, because she is his wife. When both parties uphold their responsibilities to the marriage covenant, they

---

188 The case of Ananias and Sapphira (Acts 5:1–11) provides an excellent example of this. While the two obviously conspired against God with their deceptive plan, Sapphira should have resisted her husband and refused to cooperate with his sin (cf. Acts 5:29). As it was, they perished together when they sinned together.

189 For an excellent exposition on this, I recommend *Love and Respect* by Dr. Emerson Eggerichs (Nashville: Thomas Nelson, 2004).

honor each other, the covenant itself, and the Covenant Maker. As Christ loves His church, so the husband is to love his wife: this removes all subjective interpretations on what kind of "love" Paul addresses here (see John 13:34–35).

Christ's love is a sacrificial one, since He laid down His life for His bride.[190] His *purpose* for this sacrifice is "so that He might sanctify her"—lit., make her holy (to God). Christ cannot present His bride to His Father unless she is cleansed and properly prepared. This is an ongoing process (for the physical church) and will be completed only when the entire body of believers has been assembled in the great hereafter (Heb. 12:22–24). The mode of her cleansing begins with a "washing" that agrees with (or is according to) "the word." There can be no "washing" in the NT associated with spiritual sanctification other than baptism (Acts 22:16, 1 Peter 3:21, Titus 3:4–7, and Heb. 10:19–22). The believer does his part in response to the word of God—he is "washed" with literal water. At the same time, God does His part in response to the believer's obedient faith—he (the believer) is sanctified by Christ through the Holy Spirit (1 Cor. 6:11).

In this two-fold process—his faith toward God coupled with God's supernatural work upon his soul— Christ adds the believer to His church, and the entire church itself is thus "washed" and "sanctified."[191] "[N]o spot or wrinkle" indicates a future state of the church's spiritual perfection, when the eternal wedding feast has begun (Rev. 19:7–9). The work of Christ makes this possible: He has *made* her "holy and blameless," a cleansed condition that she could not have reached on her own (Col. 1:21–22). "It was traditional for a bride to take a ritual bath just before her wedding as a symbol of her chastity. Similarly, the sacrament of baptism demonstrates the

---

190 The fact that Christ did so *before* she (the church) was made His bride shows a higher level of love than the husband who makes sacrifices for his wife *after* she has become his wife. "While we were yet sinners, Christ died for us" (Rom. 5:8)—this indicates the purest, most excellent kind of selfless love.

191 Lenski, for one, gives Christ the responsibility for our baptism: "*He* applies this means to *us, he* cleanses, etc. Baptism is *his* act and not *ours*" (*Interpretation*, 632, emphases his). This is true regarding the source of the instruction: it is by Christ's authority that every person is made a Christian through baptism. But this is not true in the literal sense: Christ did not baptize His church in water, but each person who comes into His church must do so in this manner.

Christian's desire that God should find him pure and faithful when Christ returns to claim his bride, the church."[192]

Christ, being the head of His church, loves His "body"; likewise, the husband, being the "head" of his wife, is to love her as *his* own body (5:28–31).[193] The husband's healthy love for his own body must translate to his love for his wife, since the two have become "one flesh" (Gen. 2:23–24). Christ could not have expressed to His church a kind of love He did not already have toward *Himself*, which implies that a Christian husband should have a healthy love for himself as well. No one can show love to another that he does not already have for himself. "Nourishes" and "cherishes" goes beyond the mere provision of food, clothing, and shelter. It implies the husband's tender affection toward his wife and oversight of her spiritual well-being.

The Mysterious Union of Marriage (5:31–33): "Be joined" is synonymous with being "one flesh" (5:31): the church derives her name and support from Christ, her head; likewise, the wife derives her name and support from her husband. When a man and a woman become husband and wife, the two people retain their individual identities and personalities, but they both pledge to something *transcendent* of either of them: the *new* creation of the marriage itself. From the married couple's point of view, there are three entities involved: "you," "me," and "us." What keeps these together are two essential driving forces: *devotion* and *constraint*. Devotion refers to the faithfulness based upon love and affection for the other person. Constraint refers to a sense of duty, moral obligation, and obedience to the marriage pact. Thus, when two people marry, they cannot say, "*Maybe* I do (and maybe I *don't*)," "I do (for now)," or "I do—unless you disappoint me."[194] The marriage vows are meant to be permanent. Just as Christ would never divorce His church, so the husband and wife must never even entertain the notion of dissolving their union (Mat. 19:6).

---

192 JFB, *Commentary* (electronic), on 5:27.

193 The "of His flesh, and of His bones" phrase in the KJV is "certainly not genuine" (Robertson, *Word Pictures*, 546), since it is not present in the oldest and best manuscripts for the NT. For this reason, it does not appear even as a margin reference in most modern translations or versions.

194 These points and the "me-you-us" concept are taken from Dr. Scott Stanley, *The Power of Commitment* (San Francisco: Jossey-Bass, 2005), a book I highly recommend for married couples.

"This mystery is great" (5:32)—i.e., the mysterious union between Christ and His church *and* that of a married couple's having become "one flesh." There is something transcendent and incomprehensible involved in either case. And yet, they are not equal: one is *like* the other, but the other remains *greater* than the one. Earthly marriage reflects what already exists in God's world, not the other way around. Christ's union with His church is not based upon earthly marriage, but earthly marriage is patterned after the heavenly.[195] "Nevertheless" (5:33)—i.e., even if the husband and wife do not fully comprehend this mystical union, they still are responsible to each other, the relationship itself (the "us"), and God. Thus, the husband is to love his wife unconditionally; his wife is to respect her husband's headship over their union.

Other Relationships (Eph. 6:1–9)

Instructions for Children (6:1–3): Having discussed the most important relationship that Christians enter with one another (i.e., marriage), Paul now turns his attention to the natural result of that relationship: children. "Children, obey your parents in the Lord, for this is right" (6:1). The immediate question here is: Does Paul speak only to *Christian* children, or to *all* children (of Christian parents)? A secondary question concerns the *age* of these children and begs the question of children becoming Christians at all. (In the NT, only here and in Col. 3:20 are children specifically and personally confronted with their obedience to God.) The phrase "in the Lord" seems at first to indicate Christian children, but this is not what Paul says. He does not say, "Children who are in the Lord, obey your parents," but appeals to a more general instruction based on the natural order of Creation [implied] and clearly restated in the Law of Moses (Exod. 20:12). While *all* children are to obey their parents, children of Christian parents— whether those children have become Christians themselves—must view their responsibility to God as even more important and compelling than any earthly relationship. As to the age of these children, this cannot be

---

195 "Paul has often been accused of having a low view of marriage, i.e., that non-marriage is better than marriage. But where in all the Scriptures is there a more exalted and truly spiritual conception of marriage than that presented here by this apostle?" (Lenski, *Interpretation*, 626). Robertson concurs (*Word Pictures*, 546).

determined conclusively, but by implication it must refer to those who are still living in their father's house and thus under his oversight (cf. 1 Tim. 3:4–5). A son (for example) who is no longer living with his parents is not bound to his father's house rules, yet he is *forever* bound to his moral responsibility to his parents.

"Honor your father and mother" (6:2–3) is a statement that carries no age or time implications; it is an expectation of *all* children of *all* ages. If one's parents are alive, the son or daughter is to honor them (Mark 7:9–13). "Honor" means to give respect, esteem, and (if necessary) financial support (cf. 1 Tim. 5:17). Paul cites the Ten Commandments to underscore the importance of this injunction (Exod. 20:12, Deut. 5:16). In that case, the "promise" meant that God would bless a person with a long and prosperous life who honors his parents (6:3). In the present case, there is no promise of a prolonged *or* prosperous life, but something better: an eternal fellowship with God if he continues to obey Him.

Instructions to Fathers (6:4): "Fathers, do not provoke your children to anger" (6:4). Now Paul speaks directly to the head of the household because of the authority and responsibility with which God has entrusted him. "Provoke" means to infuriate, enrage, overwhelm with frustration, or exasperate (Col. 3:21). This instruction is brief yet significant: the father's abuse of his authority or his perversion of justice (within the home) is a source of provocation for children. This would be the case if he:

- puts stumbling blocks in the (spiritual) path of his children (Mat. 18:6).
- fails to be consistent in the administration of rules, justice, rewards, or punishments.
- is a hypocrite—i.e., he portrays himself in one manner when with Christians, but in an entirely different manner when in the privacy of his home.
- makes no effort to live what he preaches to his children (Rom. 2:21–24).
- fails to prepare them for life, setting them up for future failure.
- is overprotective and does not allow his children the ability to exercise responsibility.
- is neglectful and gives little time or attention to his children.
- is abusive, either mentally or physically.

Fathers are supposed to rule (or manage) their children well (1 Tim. 3:4–5); they are to be fair, balanced, and righteous in this management. Instead of provoking their children to anger, they are to "bring them up in the discipline and instruction of the Lord"—i.e., another "not that, but this"-kind of instruction. "Discipline" involves instruction, training, nurturing, correction, and punishment (if necessary). In a big picture perspective, it refers to stability, structure, and encouragement to do what is right. The "instruction of the Lord" indicates the spiritual nature of this education (Deut. 6:7, Prov. 22:6). A father is to prepare his children to become Christians; this is his primary moral responsibility to them. This is in glaring contrast to the heathen world's treatment of its children. For example, "A Roman father had absolute power over is family. He could sell them as slaves, work them in the fields, even in chains. He could take the law into his own hand (he was the law), punish as he liked, and even inflict the death penalty on a child!"[196]

Instructions to Slaves (6:5–8): Children were barely above slaves in value in the ancient world. Slaves comprised a healthy percentage of the population of the Roman Empire. There were various classes of slavery: war captives, indentured servants, educated professionals, tradesmen, scribes, house servants, etc. These slaves were not all treated poorly, as Americans view slavery today; not all of them were enslaved against their will. On the other hand, many slaves were considered chattel, often expendable, and were at the mercy of their often unmerciful and ungodly masters.

Paul's message to Christian slaves is this: just because you have become a servant of Christ does not mean that you no longer need to serve your earthly master (6:5–8). Spiritual fellowship with Christ does not nullify or diminish one's earthly relationships; in some ways, it heightens one's sense of purpose, participation, and sincerity in those relationships. Thus, Christian slaves are to conduct themselves in a serious and respectful manner toward their masters, just as they are to conduct themselves toward Christ Himself (see Phil. 2:12 for the use of "fear and trembling" in that case). The slave's true Master is Christ, but he properly serves Christ through his earthly servitude (Col. 3:22–25). He is to work as hard for his master while he is absent as he would in his presence ("not by way of eyeservice"—6:6).

---

[196] Quoted in Coffman, *Commentary*, 234.

One's earthly master may not always see what is happening, but God sees everything and will compensate men according to their deeds (2 Cor. 5:10). The servant should seek to please God, not merely to please men (Gal. 1:10).

Instructions to Masters (6:9): Masters also are to serve God through their righteous dealings with their servants, just as servants are to do for them (6:9). In both cases, *love for God* is the prime motivation for action, but this love reveals itself in *mutual respect* and *righteous behavior*, especially among fellow brothers in Christ. From heaven's perspective, both master and servant "in Christ" are equals (Gal. 3:28, Col. 3:11); their earthly relationship is to reflect this brotherly equality, not ignore it. Just as there is "no partiality" with God (Acts 10:34–35, Rom. 2:9–11), so masters are not to show partiality toward their servants. As a father's abuse of his authority and his perversion of justice enrages and exasperates his children, so a master's abuse of *his* authority will enrage and exasperate his servants. Thus, "give up threatening"—i.e., stop menacing and provoking your slaves to anger to get them to work. Such are the ways of unconverted men but not Christian brothers.

This section on slaves and masters begs the question of slavery itself. Many believe that slavery is morally wrong; nineteenth-century abolitionists argued this position in their quest to put an end to slavery in America. Yet the NT Scripture never says slavery is wrong. Beyond what was just cited (6:5–8 and Col. 3:22–25), we should consider what else is said on this subject:

- "Each man must remain in that condition in which he was called. Were you called while a slave? Do not worry about it; but if you are able also to become free, rather do that. For he who was called in the Lord while a slave, is the Lord's freedman; likewise he who was called while free, is Christ's slave" (1 Cor. 7:20–22).
- "All who are under the yoke as slaves are to regard their own masters as worthy of all honor so that the name of God and our doctrine will not be spoken against" (1 Tim. 6:1).
- "Servants, be submissive to your masters with all respect, not only to those who are good and gentle, but also to those who are unreasonable. For this finds favor with God" (1 Peter 2:18–19).

Nowhere does the NT order masters to release their slaves, or for slaves to cease to obey their masters. On the contrary, Paul argued for the *return* of a runaway slave (Onesimus) to his owner (Philemon), but only asked his master to treat him as a brother in Christ and not merely as a slave (Phile. 15–16). (In the ancient world, masters had a legal right to punish—and even execute—slaves who disobeyed them, and especially those who abandoned them.) "Paul's instructions here did not free slaves; but, as Dummelow said, 'It freed slavery of its evils' and set in motion forces that would ultimately destroy, not only slavery, but other evil institutions as well."[197] Similarly, Lenski writes, "Christ and the apostles did not denounce slavery and call for its immediate abolition. Christianity followed a deeper, more thorough method, it undermined slavery with the spirit of Christianity by destroying it from within."[198]

Contemporary discussions on slavery often dwell upon the abuses and deprivations of slavery, which (it is argued) ought to render the practice itself immoral. Yet this is poor reasoning: we might as well argue that marriage or child-raising is immoral because people are abused and deprived in these relationships. For something to be truly *immoral*, God must make a pronouncement against it (as in Rom. 1:22–27, 1 Cor. 6:9–10, Gal. 5:19–21, etc.). He makes no such pronouncement against slavery; He merely *regulates* the conduct of those Christians who are either masters or slaves.

Furthermore, *forms* of slavery still exist today, even in modern America: employee-employer relationships; one's servitude to the military; a government's imposition upon its citizens, in the form of taxation and other financial burdens; and (most recently) citizens' enslavement to the so-called "healthcare" establishment. Even in the case of abuses and crookedness, Christians are to conduct themselves with respect, submission, and obedience (1 Peter 2:18–19). The only time a Christian cannot comply with his "master's" instruction is when it violates God's word and/or his own conscience. ("Conscience" does not refer to one's preferences or dislikes but his personal moral understanding of right and wrong.)

---

197 Coffman, *Commentary*, 237.
198 Lenski, *Interpretation*, 652.

SECTION FIVE:
THE CHRISTIAN'S STRUGGLE
WITH THE UNSEEN WORLD
(EPH. 6:10–20)

"Finally" (6:10)—after having said so much about the Christian's *walk*, now Paul needs to address the Christian's spiritual *protection*. To "be strong in the Lord … His might" obviously points to the source of the believer's strength: it is not in himself but God who has newly created him (recall 2:10). The "you" in this section is plural (as in "all of you"); Paul addresses the Ephesian church as a "corporate warrior," yet an individual response is equally required.[199] Thus, the entire church needs to be properly outfitted with divine protection; yet each member of the body also needs his individual protection.

The Full Armor of God (6:11–17): God creates and provides for every Christian a spiritual armor for going into battle, but each believer must do his part to *put it on* (6:11). ("Full armor" comes from the Greek word *panoplia*, from which we get "panoply.") The military metaphors are entirely appropriate here: Christians are engaged in an unseen, spiritual battle—one that will certainly overtake those who are unprepared for it. Just because this battle is invisible does not mean it is not real or its effects not devastating. The "schemes of the devil" are powerful, cunning, and antagonistic; we are not to downplay his ability. On the other hand, one who is properly prepared for his confrontation with Satan will not be defeated. As James says, "Submit therefore to God. Resist the devil and he will flee from you. Draw near to God and He will draw near to you" (James 4:7–8). Christ already defeated Satan at the cross, but He did not remove Satan out of the picture—not yet. He expects His disciples to arm themselves *not* with their own strength or armor but with what God alone supplies.

"For our struggle is not against flesh and blood" (6:12). The phrase "flesh and blood" indicates human power, that which is of human origin, or the context of this (human) life. Christians face something far more powerful than mere human foes; they face otherworldly adversaries that are *more*

---

199 JFB, *Commentary* (electronic), on 6:10.

powerful than any of us. Paul is making an underlying point here with the Ephesians: many of them had placed confidence in black magic, sorceries, and other practices of the occult (Acts 19:19). Their chants, spells, and magical secrets were one thing; Satan's very real power is quite another. In other words, Paul is saying, "You attempted to dabble in otherworldly power for your own gain; but the spiritual forces of wickedness are *real* and will *destroy your soul* unless you 'stand firm' against them."

Satan has a controlling interest over the hearts of the ungodly; "The whole world lies in the power of the evil one" (1 John 5:19). His government is well-organized and hierarchical. Despite this, he does not own the human world or the physical universe, and he is no match for Christ's sovereign power and authority.[200] In the end, Christ will remove him from the picture permanently. Meanwhile, Paul does not specifically define the "rulers," "powers," "forces," or manifestation(s) of "wickedness"; it would be mere conjecture for us to do so. He only says that they exist, and that they are active, predatory, and relentless (1 Peter 5:8).

Three times in this section (6:10–14) Paul uses the phrase "stand firm." Keeping with the military theme of Paul's analogy, to "stand firm" describes a soldier who holds his ground and does not surrender, retreat, or abandon his post at the presence of the enemy. Anyone can "stand firm" if there is no one challenging or assaulting him; to "stand firm" in combat is a different matter altogether. "[H]aving done everything" (6:13) indicates the need for the *full* armor, not just one piece or another; one's defense must be complete and systematic, not incidental or hit-and-miss. The "armor of God" imagery would be familiar to the Ephesians, since their mythical heroes were so outfitted by their pagan gods.[201] Likely, Paul alludes to a much more common picture: a Roman soldier who is prepared for battle (6:13–17):

- ❏ **be girded with truth.** Paul alludes to a Roman soldier's thick leather apron which covered the abdomen to the thighs. This not only offered the soldier protection, but he attached his sword's sheath to it. Paul says, in essence, "Wrap the truth around you; surround yourself with it."

---

200 See Luke 11:22, for example, where *panoplia* is also used. In that case, however, it is Christ *taking away* Satan's "full armor" and completely disarming him, thus destroying his power (see Heb. 2:14–15).
201 JFB, *Commentary* (electronic), on 6:13.

Because Satan is the "father of lies" (John 8:44), he will seek to disarm believers by deceiving them with his arsenal of lies.

- **put on the breastplate of righteousness.** A "breastplate" refers to the thick leather or metal plate strapped to the Roman soldier's chest, offering protection of his heart and other vital organs. The ancients believed that the literal heart was the seat of a man's emotions—the center of his feelings. Thus, regardless of how a Christian "feels," he must do what is right according to what God has revealed to him in His word.
- **shod your feet with the preparation of the gospel of peace.** "Peace" is the opposite of warfare; yet in a world of good and evil, men must fight wars to achieve it. The Roman soldier wore a special shoe (or sandal) that offered him protection but allowed him to maneuver easily. To "shod" the feet calls to mind two simultaneous thoughts: a footprint (or impression) as well as footing (or stability). Satan's strategy is to cause friction, discord, division, and conflicts of interest among God's people; Christians must therefore have a solid and stable footing in the truth. At the same time, they must communicate in and strive for peace, as much as it depends upon them (Mat. 5:9, Rom. 12:18, and Heb. 12:14).
- **take up the shield of faith.** The Roman soldier's shield was one of his most important forms of defense; typically, this shield was about four feet high and two feet wide, allowing him to crouch behind it when attacked by arrows, flaming darts, or other weapons. Likewise, the Christian's faith stands between him and the enemy; yet the *reason* for and *substance* of that faith rests upon the evidence God has provided *and* his conviction in that evidence (Heb. 11:1–2). Each man's faith must be constantly "supplied" (or added to) to keep it functional (2 Peter 1:5–7).
- **put on the helmet of salvation.** One's head is the most important part of his body; it is also a vulnerable target for the enemy. For these reasons, it must be sufficiently protected (1 Thess. 5:8). The head represents the source of one's thoughts and reasoning; it also alludes to the source of one's (fighting) morale. If one's thinking process is corrupted, he will not reason correctly and his conclusions will be compromised; if he has lost the will to fight, then the battle will be lost (as far as he is concerned). It is imperative that the believer's thoughts and attitude remain protected by God's promises; his courage in battle is dependent upon the confidence of his salvation (Heb. 10:35).

- ❏ **take up the sword of the Spirit.** The short, double-edged, and razor-sharp Roman sword was used offensively (to attack) as well as defensively (to protect). The one who mastered the use of this sword was an excellent fighter indeed. Similarly, the power behind the Christian "soldier" is not his own resources but his utilization of what the Spirit has provided him: the word of God. This word exposes spiritual error and destroys the "fortresses" of men (2 Cor. 10:5); it also defends against Satan's lies, temptations, and seductions. The sword is not the Spirit Himself but is what He has given us to fight against the unseen enemy. We should not think that God simply hands us our weapon and then leaves us to fight these spiritual forces of wickedness on our own. The "sword of the Spirit" is what God has given to *us*; what God does behind the scenes (and that is unknown to us) goes well beyond what we encounter.

This *one suit of armor* is ideal for *all* confrontations with Satan and his schemes. Just as God is "one," so the armor is "one": while identified by its separate parts, it remains one unit. If any parts are missing, it is not yet "the full armor of God" but remains incomplete. It is ever-ready; it is a universal, one-size-fits-all outfit that never needs to be replaced—but it *does* need to be put on every day. No Christian is too good, too smart, or too gifted to wear this; no one is exempted from putting it on. Paul does not say, "Think about the armor" or "Talk about it in Bible classes" or "Memorize its different parts." Instead, he instructs us to *learn* what this armor is and then to *put it on*. "No passage in all the Bible any more dramatically teaches the absolute necessity of the Christian's thorough knowledge of the word of God. Not having it, he is naked, barefooted, bareheaded and helpless before the enemy."[202]

The Value of Prayer (6:18–20): While not technically a part of the armor itself, prayer is nonetheless how one puts it on (6:18). This battle involves us, but it is not our battle: it is Satan's war against God, his assault against God's people. Prayer allows us to give the battle over to God rather than trying to fight it alone. Suiting up in God's armor without prayer is like handing a gun to a soldier without orders, training, battle strategy, or even identifying the enemy. Furthermore, Christians should not pray only when we see the

---

202 Coffman, *Commentary*, 242.

enemy approaching, or during an actual assault, but long before any evident confrontation. We are to be a prayerful people—devoted to prayer (Col. 4:2)—rather than merely people who say prayers. "A prayerless Christian is a contradiction of terms."[203]

"[I]n the Spirit" indicates our great reliance upon the Holy Spirit to conduct our prayers to God *and* to respond to our prayers according to Christ's direction. Not only are we to pray for ourselves (and our own battles), but also for "all the saints" and the church's collective stand against Satan. The church is not comprised of rogue warriors who fight alone but soldiers who fight the enemy and pray to God *together*. Paul so believes in the power of prayer that he solicits specific petitions regarding his own difficult circumstances (6:19–20). His responsibility is to "make known with boldness the mystery of the gospel"—i.e., to proclaim without reservation the universal salvation (recall 3:1–12). His Roman imprisonment is a direct result of this preaching; his "chains" symbolize man's feeble attempt to imprison his gospel (recall 4:1; see Acts 21:33, 26:29, 28:20 and 2 Tim. 2:8–9).[204]

Concluding Remarks (Eph. 6:21–24)

Whatever else Paul wants the Ephesians to know about his circumstances, Tychicus, one of his trusted assistants, will disclose this (6:21–22). Tychicus has been Paul's long-time companion and is a fellow minister of the gospel (see Col. 4:7–9, 2 Tim. 4:12, and Titus 3:12). Paul did not conduct all his work single-handedly but surrounded himself with capable individuals to whom he could delegate certain responsibilities. He would send these trustworthy men to different "hot spots" within the brotherhood (see Acts 20:4 for a brief list of such men; add to this Apollos, Barnabas, Crescens, Titus, Mark, Onesiphorus, and others). Tychicus would update the Ephesians concerning Paul; he would also be able to encourage and exhort

---

203 *Ibid.*, 243.

204 These "chains" refers to a singular "bond"—a single chain by which a prisoner was bound to a Roman soldier as a kind of limited custody. "Bonds" or (multiple) "chains" was used when a prisoner's hands and feet were bound together, as in Acts 26:29 (JFB, *Commentary* [electronic], on 6:20).

them according to what Paul has written, since he is likely the bearer of this epistle.

"Peace be to the brethren, and love with faith" (6:23–24). God is the Source of all peace among believers (Phil. 4:7); He is also the inspiration of all brotherly love ("We love, because He first loved us"—1 John 4:19). "Faith" is what believers demonstrate in God in response to His love and in anticipation of His peace. "Grace" refers to all that God does for the sake of His people regarding their salvation. "Incorruptible {love}"—the translators have added the word "love," as it is necessarily implied—refers to the holy manner in which believers love Christ and Christ loves His believers. Just as God is constant and "incorruptible" (Rom. 1:23), so is the love which binds together His church (Col. 3:14).

Sources Used for *Quick Study Commentary: Ephesians*

Caldwell, C. G. *Truth Commentaries: Ephesians.* Bowling Green, KY: Guardian of Truth Foundation, 1994.

Coffman, James Burton. *Commentary on Galatians, Ephesians, Philippians, Colossians.* Austin, TX: Firm Foundation, 1977.

Cogdill, Roy E. *The New Testament: Book by Book.* Marion, IN: Cogdill Foundation Publications, 1975.

Conybeare, W. J. and J. S. Howson. *The Life and Epistles of St. Paul.* Grand Rapids: Eerdmans, 1964.

Eggerichs, Dr. Emerson. *Love and Respect.* Nashville: Thomas Nelson, 2004.

Hendriksen, William. *New Testament Commentary: Galatians, Ephesians, Philippians, Colossians and Philemon.* Grand Rapids: Baker Books, 1995.

Jamieson, Robert, Andrew Fausset and David Brown. *Commentary Critical and Explanatory on the Whole Bible (1871)*, electronic edition. Database © 2012 by WORDsearch Corp.

Lenski, R. C. H. *Commentary on the New Testament (vol. 8): The Interpretation of St. Paul's Epistles to the Galatians, to the Ephesians, and to the Philippians.* Peabody, MA: Hendrickson Publishers, 1998.

Lipscomb, David. *A Commentary on the New Testament Epistles, volume IV: Ephesians, Philippians and Colossians.* J. W. Shepherd, ed. Nashville: Gospel Advocate Co., 1976.

Pickup, Jr., Harry. Class notes on Ephesians (August 2—5, 2004).

Robertson, Archibald T. *Word Pictures in the New Testament,* vol. 4. Grand Rapids: Baker Books, 1931.

Stanley, Dr. Scott. *The Power of Commitment.* San Francisco: Jossey-Bass, 2005.

Strong, James. *Strong's Talking Greek-Hebrew Dictionary*, electronic edition. Database © 2009 WORDsearch Corp.

Sychtysz, Chad. *The Holy Spirit of God: A Biblical Perspective.* Waynesville, OH: Spiritbuilding Publishers, 2010.

_____. *The New Testament Pattern: God's Plan for Christians and Their Churches*. Waynesville, OH: Spiritbuilding Publishers, 2023.

Scripture taken from the NEW AMERICAN STANDARD BIBLE ®,
Copyright © 1960, 1962, 1963, 1968, 1971, 1972, 1973, 1975, 1977, 1995
by THE LOCKMAN FOUNDATION.
Used by permission.

⇒ **End** ⇐

www.ingramcontent.com/pod-product-compliance
Lightning Source LLC
Chambersburg PA
CBHW041925090426
42743CB00020B/3440